PERFECT PICTURES

Amateur *Photographer*

GUIDE TO

PERFECT
PICTURES

BARRY MONK

HAMLYN

First published 1989 by
The Hamlyn Publishing Group Ltd
a division of the Octopus Publishing Group
Michelin House, 81 Fulham Road, London SW3 6RB
© 1989 The Hamlyn Publishing Group Ltd

ISBN 0 600 56027 9

Produced by Mandarin Offset in Hong Kong

CONTENTS

USING A CAMERA

GETTING STARTED

▼ Holding the camera horizontally feels like the most natural posture, and makes sense for subjects that run across the frame, like this row of beacons. Cropping top and bottom emphasizes the horizontal theme.

THE BASICS

Ready to go   Don't use a camera until you know what you're doing. Just as you wouldn't drive a car until you had mastered the controls, so you have to be sure of how the camera functions before 'going on the road' with it. Cameras usually look more complex than they actually are. Without the 'frills' each camera is just a box which transfers an image on to film – all you have to do is to find out how to handle it before you are ready to go out taking pictures.

Instructions   Always read the instruction booklet supplied with the camera (if it is new). With the camera in hand go through each section of the instructions and familiarise yourself with the various working functions. If you don't understand something first time around, move on to the next section and return to that part later.

Add-on accessories   Most 35mm SLRs are supported by a range of back-up accessories. Find out what lenses and accessories are available so you can develop your use of it as you become more expert. See also Equipment, pages 106-109.

Check results   After shooting and processing a roll of film, always check the results carefully. Analyse not just the quality of processing, but your own shooting style. Can you do better? Is the lighting right? Can the angles be varied for more interest? These and many factors can combine to improve your photography and reduce the wastage caused by bad shots, and save money in the long run.

Courses   There are many courses which will help you understand camera equipment and how to use it. Schools and colleges list courses locally and you can find short courses advertised in photographic magazines.

Hand held Remember that the camera is a precision tool and should be handled with care. Hold the camera firmly in both hands, with the right index finger on the shutter release. If the camera has manual controls, operate the lever wind with your right thumb, and the focusing and aperture rings with your left hand.

Horizontal/vertical Most cameras are designed to take horizontal-format pictures when held normally. This is fine for such subjects as landscapes or groups of people, but for portraits, tall buildings and so on, hold the camera vertically to include more of the subject and less of any unnecessary background.

Support When you hold the camera, tuck your elbows into the sides of your body to add extra support and to avoid camera shake spoiling your pictures. You can also support the camera on a wall or any similar nearby surface.

Tripod The best way to achieve shake-free pictures is to mount the camera on a tripod – see page 15.

Lying down If you lie on your stomach, you can support the camera with your elbows resting firmly on the ground. This supports the camera, but also allows you a certain amount of movement.

The right film Before shooting make sure you have a film in the camera – even the most expert photographers forget sometimes! Also check that you have the right film before putting it in the camera. Some cameras have a film memo holder on the back – cut off one end of the film carton and place it in the holder. This will remind you which type of film was used.

Enprints Most labs crop off some of the frame when printing, so leave plenty of space around the subject when shooting negative film.

Camera settings Check the camera settings before you start taking photographs. In particular, make sure the correct ISO film speed has been set. See the rest of this section for other important settings.

Using the viewfinder Simpler cameras show in the viewfinder more of the subject than appears on film: a bright frame outlines the picture area, so keep the subject within these lines. With an SLR, compose the picture within the entire area of the viewfinder.

Heads and feet Look at the frame edges when composing the picture to make sure you're not cutting off heads or feet. The viewfinders of simple cameras have small marks on the top of the bright frame to show the safe limit for close-ups. Anything above the marks will not appear.

▲ Turning the camera so that the longer side of the frame runs vertically demands a more awkward posture, but makes much more satisfying compositions with predominantly vertical subjects.

▲ Don't restrict
yourself to subject
matter that is
traditionally regarded
as picturesque. The
off-beat and unusual
can make dramatic
and stylish
compositions, too.
Shooting from a low
viewpoint here
isolated the beacon
against a colourful sky,
and cut out urban
clutter in the
background.

Simple cameras
keep more of the
subject sharp in bright
light than on dull days.
In sunlight, you may
be able to move
closer to your subject
than the camera
instructions suggest.
Experiment first
before risking this
technique with
important subjects.

Backgrounds When you are shooting a portrait don't forget the background. Look at the detail behind the subject before pressing the shutter release. If there is a tree appearing to 'grow' out of the subject's head, or any unnecessary clutter in the background, ask the sitter to move, or change your shooting position. Check the whole viewfinder area, not just the part occupied by the main subject.

Composing Learning how to compose pictures is one of the most important aspects of photography. You can learn a great deal by simply looking at other photographs (in magazines, newspapers, books and so on). Look at the key elements of each picture, how it was put together, and the general framing of the shot. Quite often, impact relies not on what is in a picture, but what is left out. Avoid clutter – a simple approach usually works best.

Changing viewpoint Don't stay in the same position when you are taking pictures. Move around and try different viewpoints. Don't just shoot a portrait head-on: photograph from the side, or from above or below as well. In a landscape, avoid the obvious view and try shooting from a high vantage point (like a hill), or walk around until you find a different angle.

Focusing Most new cameras set the focusing automatically, so that pictures are almost always sharp. With these cameras, all you need do to focus is to make sure the most important part of the subject is centred in the viewfinder, then lightly depress the shutter release. If you want the subject central, just press harder to take the picture, but if you want an off-centre subject, simply maintain light pressure while you turn the camera to make a different composition. Further pressure then operates the camera's shutter. Older autofocus cameras may not have this 'focus hold' feature.

Autofocus problems Some subjects and lighting conditions can 'fool' autofocus cameras. The commonest example is a double portrait with a distant view behind: the camera 'looks' between the figures and focuses on the background. The solution is simple – turn the camera so that one face is centred in the viewfinder, lightly press the shutter release to focus, then hold focus as outlined earlier, while you recompose the picture. With

autofocus SLRs, dim light can cause problems, too. In very dark conditions, you may have to focus manually or fit a special flash unit that projects a pattern onto the subject, so that the camera can focus normally.

Manual focusing With non-autofocus SLRs, you need to turn the focusing ring until the image in the viewfinder looks sharp. If you find this hard to judge, use the circular focusing aid in the middle of the screen. The line crossing the circle displaces unsharp subjects, so they appear 'broken': turning the focusing ring aligns the two halves.

Focusing aids A few of the more costly SLR cameras have interchangeable focusing screens. If you have trouble focusing manually, it may be worthwhile trying a different screen.

▼ With distant scenes where none of the subject matter is close to the camera, manual-focus cameras can be set to infinity. There's no need to change the focus setting between pictures.

UNDERSTANDING EXPOSURE

What is exposure? All film needs just the right amount of light to make a good picture, and cameras control the quantity of light reaching the film in two ways: the size of the *aperture* controls the *brightness* of the light entering the camera; and the *shutter* controls *how long* the image from the lens falls on the film. Many cameras set both aperture and shutter automatically, so you have no manual control over exposure, and you can skip the next few paragraphs. However, if your camera has a 'manual' option, you'll need to know a little about shutter speed and aperture if you are to use the camera to its full potential.

Apertures   The size of the aperture is adjusted manually using a ring on the lens, or a button on the camera body. The control is calibrated with 'f-numbers' which indicate the size of the aperture you've chosen. Confusingly, the scale begins with low numbers which mark large apertures – on most good cameras f/1.4 or f/1.8 marks the widest aperture. Smaller apertures get bigger numbers in a standard sequence – 2, 2.8, 4, 5.6, 8, and so on, to 22 or beyond. Each setting lets through twice as much light as the next higher number, and half as much as the adjacent setting with a lower number. Aperture doesn't just affect exposure: at small apertures, there's more depth of field: things in front of and behind the subject on which you've focused appear sharper on film.

Shutter speed   This is not really a speed in the common sense, but a time: the shutter speed indicates how long the shutter is open as a fraction of a second, and again, each successive setting lets half as much light reach the film: 1/60, for example, lets through half as much light as 1/30, and twice as much as 1/125. On most adjustable cameras, the shutter speed runs from a full second to 1/1000, though there may additionally be faster and slower speeds. Like aperture, shutter speed has an extra function: subjects that move while the shutter is open look blurred on film, so if you want to stop action, you need to set faster speeds.

Film speed   Again, this isn't a speed, but photo-jargon for the sensitivity of the film to light, and it's indicated by the ISO number printed on the film packet. 'Fast' films with high ISO numbers have a high sensitivity to light, so you can use fast shutter speeds and/or small apertures to stop action, or keep more of the subject sharp. 'Slow' films have low ISO numbers, and a lower sensitivity. With slow films you must use slower shutter speeds and wider apertures, but in compensation, colours and other picture qualities are likely to be better. Don't be confused if you see film speed expressed as an ASA value instead of ISO – the older ASA system is exactly equal to ISO.

Setting film speed   Many 35mm cameras set film speed automatically, using the DX code – the pattern of silver and black squares on the cassette. If your camera does not have the necessary contacts in the cassette chamber, you'll need to set film speed manually, on a special dial. Read your camera's instructions to find where this is located.

The camera's meter   Set to 'programmed auto exposure', the meter in your camera measures the light reflected from the subject, and sets the aperture and shutter to values that will give correct exposure with the film in use. For casual picture taking, this system is hard to beat, and indeed with many cameras this is the only exposure option available. However, with unusual subjects and for special effects, you may instead want to switch to one of the following exposure modes, if they are available on your camera.

Speed program   At this setting, the camera chooses the fastest possible shut-

▼ Sunsets can fool the meters in even the most sophisticated cameras. To set exposure, take a meter reading from an area of sky adjacent to the sun, but exclude the sun itself from the frame. Then either set the camera manually, or use the exposure lock button as outlined in the text.

If your camera does not lock on to an automatic setting, make sure you don't knock the control manually when shooting. Use sticky tape to keep the control still.
Don't keep to one exposure setting in changeable weather. If the light varies, so should your settings for accurate results.

CRYSTAL PALACE

▲ You'll get less blurred pictures at any shutter speed if the subject is approaching the camera, rather than crossing the frame.

an appropriate aperture. A viewfinder warning will light if you choose a shutter speed that is so fast or slow that no available aperture will yield good exposures.

Depth program This is the reverse of the speed program: the camera sets a shutter speed just fast enough to eliminate camera shake, then picks the smallest aperture that will give correct exposure. This approach increases depth of field, so there is more of the subject in focus behind and in front of the sharpest areas.

Aperture priority Aperture priority metering hands control of the aperture over to the photographer. You choose the aperture, and the camera picks a shutter speed that will give correct exposure. As with shutter priority, the camera warns if you make an error.

Manual metering Setting the camera to 'manual' puts you fully in control, so it's the best choice for subjects that might fool a camera set to 'auto'. In manual mode, you point the camera at the subject, and take a meter reading – usually by pressing the shutter release gently. The camera then gives some indication of whether the aperture and shutter speed you've chosen will produce correct exposure. The indication may be glowing arrows or figures, a liquid crystal display (LCD) as on a wrist watch, or even an old-fashioned meter needle. You can then change either of the controls until the camera signals that exposure is correct.

Other exposure controls Exposure lock freezes the camera's exposure settings while you hold the control down. Exposure lock is useful if you are photographing subjects set against backgrounds that are very dark or light. You can close in, meter the subject, hold down the exposure lock while you back off, then recompose the picture – without losing the meter reading.

ter speed, and wide apertures, so it's the best exposure mode when you want to freeze moving subjects.

Shutter priority This mode gives more control over shutter speed: you pick the speed manually, and the camera chooses

▲ Backlighting misleads the camera's meter, producing underexposure. To retain detail in this portrait, the photographer gave one stop more exposure than a meter reading suggested.

Backlighting When photographing someone with the camera facing the sun, the camera meter is likely to expose for the bright background rather than the subject's face, which is in shadow. You can increase the exposure manually by using a wider aperture to compensate (say, from f/8 to f/5.6). Some cameras, however, have an exposure compensation, or backlight control (with a range of about ±2 f/stops) for dealing with this kind of difficult lighting situation.

Depth-of-field scale You can check the area of sharpness at a particular aperture by looking at the depth-of-field scale marked on the lens, near the aperture control. Two aperture scales (minimum to maximum) meet at a middle mark. Focus the camera lens on the subject and you will see the distance opposite this mark. If you have set the camera to, say, f/16, read off the distances opposite the two f/16 marks to find out the depth-of-field range.

Depth-of-field preview You don't have to guess how much of the picture area will appear sharp if your camera has a depth-of-field preview button. First, compose and focus the shot then, while pressing in the DOF preview button on your camera, select different apertures and watch how the background detail becomes more or less sharp at each aperture. Once you are happy with a particular aperture, release the DOF preview control and shoot.

Misleading subjects The meter in the camera is calibrated to give correct exposure with 'average' subjects. Average means a uniform mid-tone – not very dark or very light – or a mixture of tones with equal amounts of dark and light. If you encounter subjects that don't fit this description, you'll need to give the film more or less exposure than the meter indicates.

Adjusting exposure Very light subjects, such as snow scenes, mislead the camera into giving too little exposure; the camera sets too fast a shutter speed, or too small an aperture and the snow comes out looking grey on film. You can correct the underexposure in several ways: the simplest is to use the exposure compensation dial if your camera has one. Set the dial to +1 (sometimes marked as ×2) to give one 'stop' of extra exposure to fairly light subjects such as pale sand. Give two extra stops by setting the dial to +2 (or ×4) for very light scenes such as sunlit snow. Alternatively, set the ISO dial to half the nominal film speed for one extra stop of exposure, or a quarter for two stops. The third way of increasing exposure is to simply set the camera to manual mode, and use a shutter speed one or two settings slower than the camera suggests, or an aperture one or two stops wider. Dark subjects need the opposite treatment: very dark pine trees, for example, may need a stop or two less than the meter indicates.

Exposure 'insurance' For very important pictures, experienced photographers

Wide apertures produce less sharp pictures than moderate apertures: try not to use a lens at full aperture.

often 'bracket' exposure. They take several pictures – one at the indicated exposure, then others with a stop or so more or less exposure than the meter indicates.

Speed effects The shutter speed you select will affect the final result, so take care to choose the right one for the subject. While 1/125 second is about right for most static subjects, shooting fast action or movement at that speed could leave you with a blurred picture, because it isn't fast enough to 'freeze' the action. In some cases, however, a small amount of blur can give the *impression* of movement.

SHUTTER SPEED TABLE

Subject	Shutter speed (second)
Portrait	1/60
Landscape	1/60
Children	1/125
People walking	1/125
Running/cycling	1/250
Medium-pace sport (e.g. football)	1/500
Fast action (e.g. car racing)	1/1000

In the case of a moving subject, these suggested speeds should be enough to 'freeze' the action. For subjects moving *towards* the camera (rather than *across* the field of view) you may be able to go down by one speed (say, from 1/125 second to 1/60 second). Results can vary depending on the distance of the subject. Generally, the closer the subject, the faster the speed should be to reduce the risk of a blurred picture.

Camera shake Many amateur pictures are spoilt by camera shake. First, use a sensible shutter speed if hand-holding the camera (no slower than 1/60 second). Second, hold the camera firmly until *after* the shot has been taken. Third, press the shutter release button gently – jabbing at it will shake the camera. Ideally, for completely shake-free exposures, place the camera on a firm support (like a tripod) and use a cable release, attached to the shutter release button on the camera, to fire the camera.

Freezing action You can see from the shutter speed table that, the faster the movement of the subject, the faster the shutter speed should be to 'freeze' the action. The speed you choose is often dictated by the amount of light available and it isn't always possible to select the fast speed you want. In low light, use the widest aperture you can (say, f/2.8) and the fastest shutter speed compatible.

▼ Electronic flash produces such a brief pulse of light that even rapid subjects hardly move while the flash illuminates them. So to catch speeding subjects – on the river-bank or in the family garden – take pictures at night and use flash.

Standard view The standard lens on your camera is designed to cover most situations. You can use a standard lens for portraits, landscapes, groups, and so on. SLR cameras have interchangeable lenses but it's wise to become familiar with the standard lens before adding any other type of lens to your equipment.

Other lenses Fitting a new lens to an SLR is similar to fitting a new window in your home: a wide-angle lens is like a picture window that gives a broader view of the world outside. A telephoto lens takes in a smaller field of view – as does a smaller window – but unlike a window, a telephoto lens magnifies the scene, so that distant things appear nearer.

Focal length The effect of a lens is indicated by its focal length, which is marked on the lens barrel. Wide-angle lenses have short focal lengths such as 28mm. Telephoto lenses have focal lengths longer than 50mm standard lens, and dividing the focal length by 50 indicates how much the lens magnifies the subject compared to the standard lens. A 200mm lens, for example, magnifies 4 times. Zoom lenses offer a variety of focal lengths over a range. For example, a 70-210mm zoom magnifies the subject by any factor you choose within the range 1.4× to 4.2×.

Wide angle lenses Choose a wide angle lens to cram more into the picture. Indoors, a wide-angle allows you to show the whole room instead of just a corner. Outside, the lens lets you fit the whole of a building in even when the obstructions prevent you from backing off and taking the picture with a standard lens. Wide angle lenses affect perspective, too, emphasizing the foreground detail, and making the background recede.

Telephoto lenses A telephoto lens acts like a telescope, pulling in distant detail that would be too small if you photo-

graphed it with a standard lens. But telephotos have a more subtle effect, too. They compress perspective, so that, for example, rows of cars on a road appear almost stacked on top of one another.

Lenses and distortion Wide-angle lenses sometimes seem to distort the subject. When you fit a wide-angle and tilt the camera up, parallel lines – such as the sides of a building – seem to converge. The solution is to keep the camera level, and perhaps seek a higher viewpoint. Another distortion occurs at the edges of the picture. Here a wide angle lens can stretch and elongate objects. So keep important detail – such as faces, away from the frame edges, and especially the corners.

Camera shake is exaggerated by telephoto lenses. Take special care to support the camera when using long focal length lenses, or telephoto zooms.

◀ Telephoto lenses allow you to fill the frame with far-off subjects, and from a distant viewpoint, normal perspective effects are minimized. In this picture, taken with a 300mm lens, the photographer chose an elevated viewpoint to spread the bandsmen across the frame, separating the figures and further heightening the sense of depth compression.

▼ When it's essential that the uprights in a picture – such as the sides of this window-frame – remain parallel, take care to keep the camera horizontal. If you don't have a tripod that you can level, check that the lines remain parallel to the edges of the viewfinder frame.

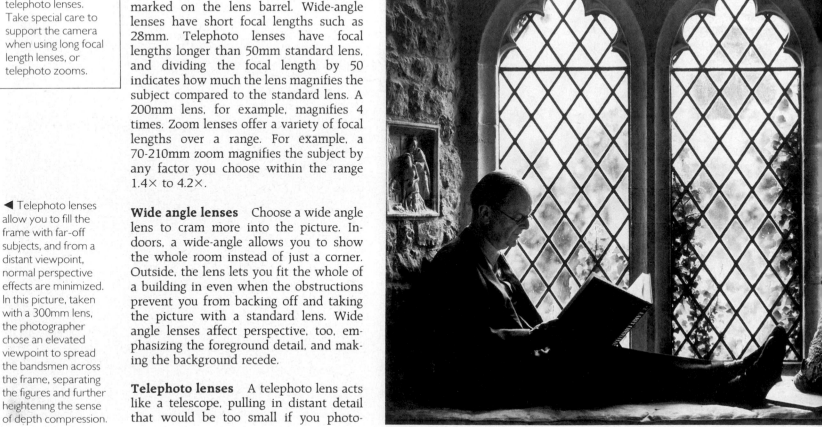

USING LIGHT

Light sources Light is essential to all photography and the camera user has a choice of different types of light sources, both natural and artificial. Daylight can provide the most natural and pleasing results, but you can use lamps or flash as alternatives, depending on your style of photography. Remember, the quality of your photography will depend as much on your skill in using light as on how you use your equipment.

Natural light Daylight is the most natural light source for photography – and it can offer the photographer an extremely wide range of effects. The quality and direction changes all the time, depending on the time of day, and year, the weather, and so on.

Bright sunlight Many photographers believe that bright sunlight is best for taking pictures. This can be so – but it also creates problems, such as very harsh shadows. Mid-morning or afternoon is better than midday for this reason. Don't photograph someone with the sun over your shoulder – harsh lighting and a squinting subject don't make a good portrait. Shoot from the side or with the camera facing the sun.

Diffused light Many photographers agree that diffused sunlight, with the sun's rays passing through thin cloud, is ideal for pictures. The light is bright enough for good results, yet the diffused effect reduces the harsh shadows experienced in direct sunlight. On a bright day watch for occasional cloud cover and try shooting when the sun is diffused by it.

▼ In windy weather with broken cloud, light changes very rapidly – and these are arguably the best conditions for landscape pictures. Be prepared to spend some time waiting for the light to change, but then work quickly, or you could miss those brief moments when the sun breaks through.

Cloudy weather   You might not get very bright results in cloudy weather, but you can get some interesting results on an overcast day. A sky heavy with clouds can look very dramatic in a landscape shot, for instance. You might need a fast film when heavy clouds cause the light level to drop.

Snow and showers   Even the most un-interesting scene can be totally trans-formed into good picture material when bad weather strikes. Rain and snow show-ers can be particularly dramatic, so don't scurry for shelter until you have tried to take a few shots. Shoot under an umbrella or from a nearby covered position if you are worried about getting your equipment soaked.

Time of day   Choosing the right time of day to take a picture is important because the quality and direction of the light given out by the sun will affect your results. You can chart this yourself by setting aside a day to photograph a nearby scenic land-scape. Start very early (around dawn) and take pictures at hourly intervals until dusk (take a packed meal and something to read in between shots). Shoot on colour film and look at the results carefully after processing. Note how the colour, direction and general effect of the lighting varies throughout the day and use this informa-tion for future reference.

Midday sun   Try to avoid taking pictures in the midday sun. Because the sun is at its highest point at this time of day, practically any subject you photograph will appear to be very flatly lit, with very small shadows which make the subject look uninteresting, or perhaps very harsh shadows. Portraits are particularly difficult to shoot in midday light.

Time of year   The effect of natural light changes with the seasons. A scene taken in spring, for example, will look very different when photographed in winter snow. Keep a record of these changes by

returning to shoot the same scene on different days during each season. Apart from weather effects, note how the quality of the light varies throughout the year.

At night   You can make an urban scene appear much more dramatic by taking pictures at night. The best time to shoot is around dusk when there is some colour detail in the sky, but the lights from streets and buildings are also visible. Use a fast film (ISO 400-plus) to keep exposure times as short as possible.

Light sources at night   When shooting night shots in colour, remember that most daylight balanced slide films will not be suitable for recording street lighting. The results will have an overall orange cast. Either use a colour correction filter over the lens (80A) or use negative film, and ask the lab to make colour corrections when they print.

Moonlight   Shooting scenes under moonlight calls for the use of a very fast film (ISO 1000) and long exposures. Re-sults will vary depending on the reflect-ivity of the scene (from buildings, water, and so on) and the brightness of the moon. Shoot under a full moon only for best results. When photographing the moon itself, exposures can be short.

▲ Misty weather softens the light and simplifies the subject into shades of grey. And where an attractive foreground is marred by an ugly urban backdrop, you can use the fog like a curtain, to hide the distant distractions.

Roads and motorways can be brightened up when the sun has set by using a long exposure. Wait until your meter indicates an exposure of ten seconds or longer, then lock the shutter open for double the indicated time. Lights from passing cars will leave attractive coloured trails.

Take a small torch along for night shots so you can see what settings you are making on the camera controls.

▲ Remember that the sun moves across the sky in the course of the day: this picture, taken close to noon, would have been disappointing had it been taken early or late in the day.

Window light Daylight coming through a window (or doorway) can provide a very appealing light for portraits. Avoid direct sunlight, which throws awkward shadows. Shoot on bright, but slightly cloudy, days or look for a north facing window.

Reflector One useful and economical accessory for window-light portraits is a reflector. While lighting one side of the subject's face from the window, the other side is cast in shadow. A reflector held on this side will reflect back the light and give a more even lighting effect. The reflector can be a piece of white card, a sheet, or even a newspaper. You can also buy a special fold-out reflector which is called a Lastolite.

Lamp light You can often shoot indoors using ordinary household lights providing you have a reasonably fast film in the camera. Avoid using overhead lights when photographing people because of the awkward shadows they cast – but they are fine for interior room shots. Table lamps or spotlights can be used for portraits but you may need to use a reflector to fill-in shadow areas. With colour slide film balanced for daylight, you must use a correction filter (80A) or use tungsten balanced film for accurate colour rendition. With negative film, the lab should make the necessary adjustment when they print.

Can the film cope? In very low light, where very long exposures are needed, films (particularly colour) may suffer what is called *reciprocity failure*. This means that even after giving the 'correct' exposure, the picture may still be underexposed, and colours in the photograph may be very strange.

Using reflection Always be aware of the effect of reflected light. In a scene, light reflected from glass (in buildings) and water (lakes, fountains, etc.) can add sparkle to your pictures. Light reflected off

In dim light the simplest tactics are often the most effective: if the camera indicates a shutter speed too slow to hand-hold, try moving your subject closer to the light source.

Using the existing light You don't always need flash to shoot pictures indoors. With today's fast films, the light already there, whether it is daylight from a window, a door or even a skylight, or artificial light, may be quite bright enough for a picture. Even if your camera has built-in flash, using the existing light can often give a more natural-looking and attractive photograph than using flash.

strongly coloured surfaces can affect the colours in your main subject. If you photograph someone in a bright green outfit, for instance, green reflections may appear in the person's face, possibly spoiling the shot. Use reflections to your advantage – a dramatic sky or landscape can have twice the impact if it is also reflected in a lake.

Reflected flare Make sure reflections from, or around, the subject being photographed don't cause 'flare' spots to appear in the lens. Flare can be a particular problem when photographing water or glass. A lens hood can reduce flare from outside the picture area, or a polarising filter will help reduce reflection in the subject area.

Light direction With any type of light, (from daylight to candlelight), the direction it comes from, and how it hits the subject, dictate the final effect. Try to vary the direction of the lighting in your photography and see how the results change. If you can't move the light source (as in daylight photography) move around with the camera or alter the position of the subject you are photographing.

▼ Direct sun through a window creates harsh shadows. When detail is important, keep your subject out of the sun and rely on reflected sunlight for illumination.

► For good pictures by candlelight, shoot when the subject's face is close to the flames, since the light falls off rapidly with distance. Keep the flames themselves out of the frame when you take a meter reading, or your pictures will be underexposed.

Never be caught out by failing flash batteries. Have at least one spare set handy.

Candlelight   To take pictures in candle-light you need a fast film (at least ISO 200, and preferably ISO 1000) and a longish exposure. With daylight-balanced slide film the effect will be warm or orangey, but this often enhances the natural effect of candlelight. Remember to keep the subject close to the candle flame.

Flash lighting   The most portable and easy to use form of lighting is flash. You can use an on-camera flash unit for most pictures and larger studio units are avail-able for home studio work.

Right connection   If your camera has a hot shoe connection (which is usually found on top of the camera) you can fit, and fire, practically any portable flash unit. Otherwise connect the flash via a sync lead (supplied with most flash units) to the X-sync socket on the camera (see also page 67).

Synchronization   If flash is to illuminate the subject properly, the shutter must be fully open at the exact moment when the flash fires. Most SLR cameras have a fixed maximum shutter speed for using flash marked with an X on the shutter speed dial. Don't exceed it.

Automatic flash   Used with a dedicated flash unit, most modern cameras take care of flash exposure without any need for calculations.

Manual settings   When using a manual flashgun with no automatic settings, set the film speed in use on the calculator dial. Look at the distance scale and, opposite the particular distance your camera is away from the subject, read the required lens aperture on the f/stop scale. Using ISO 100 film, for example, the dial may suggest you use an aperture of f/8 with the subject 3 metres (10ft) away.

Print film tolerates even quite severe errors of colour balance – so if you're shooting negatives, you needn't bother with colour correction filters except for pictures where an exact colour match is vital.

Remember that you can soften direct lighting with a diffuser.

Auto settings Unlike manual flash, where the full power of the flash is used each time you shoot, a flash set on automatic emits just the right amount of light for the subject, thus saving power for subsequent shots. Most auto flash units offer a choice of three or four auto settings, depending on which lens aperture you choose to work at. Set the ISO film speed on the dial and check the subject distance against the range of auto apertures on the dial. Set the lens *and* the flash unit to the selected aperture indicated (say f/11).

Guide numbers The guide number (GN) of a flashgun can be used for manual exposure calculation, and it also indicates the maximum light output of the unit – useful when comparing different flashguns. The GN is the flash-to-subject distance (in metres) multiplied by the aperture needed for a correct exposure using ISO 100 film. For a unit of GN 16, for example, set f/8 on the lens for a subject at 2 metres (6½ft) from the flash.

Flash angles With built-in flash the light is directed straight at the subject. Many portable units now have adjustable heads which allow you to point the light in a number of different directions for better lighting effect.

Direct flash For the brightest flash effect point the flashgun straight at the subject. Most flashguns are designed to produce their best results within about 1 to 3 metres (3 to 10ft) with direct flash, so try not to go beyond this range.

Bounce effect Most lighting we see in our daily lives is overhead, from the sky outdoors and from ceiling lights indoors. Duplicate this lighting by tilting the flashgun upwards – some models have a swivel head to allow this. Alternatively, take the flash off the camera and, with its lead attached to the X-sync socket, try bouncing the light this way.

No shadows One advantage when photographing someone with direct flash is that it does not cast shadows on the face. However, be careful not to place the subject too close to the background otherwise a shadow of the person's head may be thrown, causing an unsightly black surround.

Diffused flash You can soften the effect of direct flash by using a diffuser over the front of the unit. You can buy special diffuser accessories to fit some flashguns, but a handkerchief, or similar translucent material, held over the flash tube will soften the light output. You can expect to have to increase exposure by up to one f/stop to compensate for the diffusion of the light.

Flash with daylight Don't always save your flash for indoor work. Even in bright sunlight a flash can be used effectively to fill-in harsh shadows. Some of the Polaroid instant picture cameras have automatic sunlight fill-in flash for better results.

▼ Subjects in open shade on a sunny day often appear tinted blue, because they are lit mainly by the sky. Using flash solves the problem, and puts back the sparkle in portraits. With negative film, exposure compensation is rarely needed: just switch on the flash, and set the shutter no faster than the flash synchronization speed.

Movement is easy to suggest if you mix flash and daylight: just set a shutter speed slower than 1/8, use flash and pan to follow the subject.

Program flash If your SLR has a program flash setting, you can take fully automatic flash pictures using a compatible flash unit. This is usually produced by the camera manufacturer as an optional accessory. The camera and flashgun work together to calculate a correct exposure for each flash shot, without the need for you to make any manual settings.

Freezing motion Flash light is emitted at such a fast rate that it can have the effect of 'freezing' the fastest-moving subject – even if you are shooting with a slow shutter speed.

Recycling Once you take a flash shot, remember that the flashgun has to recharge itself. How long this recycling takes depends on the type and condition of the batteries, the amount of light emitted in the last shot, and so on. Wait until the 'ready' light indicates full charge before taking another shot, otherwise under-exposure may occur.

Slave units To provide lighting from several directions at once, in a portrait for instance, use extra flashguns, making sure each is fitted with a slave unit. These tiny light-sensitive cells automatically fire any attached flashguns when the main flash, connected to the camera, goes off (see page 107).

Fill-in flash To use fill-in flash outdoors in bright sun first take a normal light reading of the subject and set the required apertures. Then, if you have an automatic flashgun, set the unit to two stops *wider* than this aperture. For example, with the lens set at f/16, the flash should be set to f/8 to produce just a touch of light to fill-in shadows. With too much flash light the subject would be far too bright and the background would darken. With a manual flashgun, set to quarter-power (if it has this facility), or cover the flash tube with a handkerchief or other piece of cloth to reduce the light output.

Light balance Flash and daylight can be mixed together in the same shot, but it takes some practice to get the right balance between the two. It is worthwhile setting up a flash/daylight shot and trying a number of different exposures and flash outputs. Keep a note of these and refer back to them when you are tackling a similar set up later.

Day to night When photographing someone in daylight you can simulate night by using full power flash at a small aperture about (f/16). Using the flash will reduce the effect of daylight and darken any natural light in the picture.

Stained glass Never use flash to photograph stained glass in a window or door – it will 'kill' the colour of the panes by ruining the effect of natural daylight filtering through the coloured glass. Take a light reading of the stained glass in daylight with a meter and then expose in the normal way.

Large areas You can photograph a large interior with a small flashgun. With the camera on a firm tripod, set the shutter to the open 'B' position and an aperture of around f/11 or f/8. (You need a locking cable release, press in the cable to open the shutter and lock the release tight – when you want to close the shutter, release the lock.) If the camera has a T-shutter position, set it and press the shutter once to open it. Then, with a flashgun in your hands, move around the area being photographed, firing the flash off in different directions. This has the effect of 'painting' light over the entire subject area. Afterwards, return to the camera to close the shutter.

Neon signs Don't use flash to photograph neon signs or similar bright light sources. The effect of the flash will cancel out the light which is emitted from the sign. Just meter and photograph in the normal way.

▶ Fill-in flash draws attention to foreground detail. Here the photographer shot from a car, using flash to pick out brilliant highlights in the shiny bike, and to throw light into the deep shadows cast by the helmet. A prismatic filter heightens the sense of speed.

Colour & Black and White

WORKING WITH COLOUR

Understanding colour Most photographers shoot colour – but few fully understand how colour works, and how it can be manipulated to produce the very best results. Looking at colour work in books and exhibitions, and deciding for yourself how colour has added impact to the image can be surprisingly helpful.

Primary colours Be aware of the way colours are reproduced on film. Colour film works by recording light in three basic colours – red, green and blue. These are called 'additive' primaries because they can be added or mixed together in various proportions to give any other colour; all three mixed together give white light. But the colours in the processed photograph are reproduced using dyes in three different basic colours – yellow, magenta (a reddy blue colour) and cyan (greeny blue). These colours are called 'subtractive' primaries because the dyes act like filters and each of the dyes gets its colour by filtering out (subtracting) either red, green or blue light. Mixing all three dyes together blocks out all light, giving black.

Colour in the subject Look for appealing colour in your subjects. A splash of bright, vibrant colour can catch the eye and add a little sparkle to even the dullest scene. But remember that subtle, pastel colours can also be attractive.

Warm colour Many photographic situations can produce results which are warm or 'orangey' in tone. Examples include a landscape photographed at sun-down, when the light confers a warm ambience. Shooting in lamplight or candlelight also produces a warm effect, if you shoot with daylight-balanced slide film.

Cool colour Shots taken on cloudy days, or in the shade, tend to have a cool bluish tinge. With negative film, the lab should correct this when printing. With slide film, fit an 81B filter to 'warm' the light, or use the colouring creatively.

Colour and mood Colour can be a great

Mixing colours may not be the best way to make good pictures on colour film. Try to use a limited number of hues in a picture – too many colours often looks garish.

► Warm colours such as reds, yellows and oranges, "advance" towards the viewer. When you juxtapose them with a cool background in blue or green hues, the picture takes on almost three-dimensional qualities.

► Ironically, some of the most effective colour pictures are almost devoid of colour. Turn the camera to face the light, and you can make even a brightly coloured scene into a symphony of subtle hues.

▲ Brilliant colours create a lively, sense of fun – hence their widespread use in fairground paintwork. To catch the colours at their brightest, shoot in direct sunlight.

mood setter, introducing another dimension into your pictures. Bright reds and yellows often give a lively, vibrant mood; pale greens a more relaxed feel. You can change the impact of a set by adding a particular colour, using props, or a filter.

Dominating colour You can create a strong effect by having just one dominant colour in the picture. A close-up of a bright red flower, for instance, can be very effective. Watch for colours that dominate a picture too heavily – the same flower in a general landscape might distract the eye from other parts of the picture.

Mixing colour Always do this with caution, and take into account the mix of colours when taking a shot. In some cases it is desirable to combine colours which go together well, with no discordant colour spoiling the impact.

Colour interest   Quite often the pattern in a colour photograph is as important as the colour itself. Look for natural colour pattern in subjects, or introduce a pattern yourself. In a portrait, for example, a bright patterned scarf or a piece of clothing with strong texture can add a great deal of extra interest to the composition.

Complementary colours   Choose colours which complement each other if you possibly can. A bad mix of colours can ruin the effect you are trying to produce. For example, a yellow rose photographed in autumn will look lost against a selection of other roses or trees with lots of yellow leaves, but a low-angled shot that placed it against blue sky instead would be pleasing.

Colour saturation   This is the depth of colour in a photograph. Colour saturation can depend on several factors, including the strength of colour in the subject, the lighting, and even the type of film. But with slide film, the most important factor is exposure. If the slide is even slightly overexposed, or the light falling on the subject is very bright, colours will be pale and washed out. To give maximum saturation with slide film, some photographers deliberately underexpose by half an aperture stop – or 'fool' the camera by setting the film speed 50% too fast.

Colour variations   You can shoot the strongest colours in good sunlight. However, overcast and cloudy weather has the effect of scattering light and thus reducing the impact of the colours in a scene. A foggy or moist atmosphere can produce an overall soft blue cast.

Dawn and dusk   You can shoot good colour throughout the day but many

Simple colour pictures dominated by a single hue are easier to take with a telephoto. With wide angle lenses it's difficult to crop out distracting subjects of other colours.

▶ Primary colours look brighter still if you frame them against a colourless background, such as the grey glass of this Manhattan skyscraper.

photographers find dawn and dusk are the best times. With the sun low in the sky there is a warm directional light which enhances practically any subject, from portrait to landscape. The sky at sunrise or sunset is particularly dramatic in colour, especially if there are interesting cloud formations.

Diffusing colour   You can deliberately soften colour in a variety of ways. Use a haze or soft-focus filter over the lens, or smear some Vaseline over a filter for a similar effect. It can be wiped off later with a lens-cleaning cloth. Be careful not to smear the lens itself. Shoot through a window covered with dust or condensation, or place a slightly patterned piece of glass in front of the lens to scatter the light.

Exposing slide film   Shooting on colour-slide film requires very accurate exposure to give good results. Even a small error in exposure can lead to poor results (see also Colour Saturation).

Exposing colour negative/print film This type of film is more tolerant of exposure errors than slide film and many mistakes can usually be corrected at the printing stage. Underexposure creates a thin, washed out negative, while over-exposure produces a dark negative. However, the latter can produce better stronger colours in the print. Some camera meters are deliberately set to overexpose for this reason.

Muted colour   Where strong colour is high in impact, muted colour is more subtle – but it can be very expressive. Look for muted colour in most natural landscapes, in grey urban environments, and so on. Remember that colour is muted by the addition of black and grey tones in a picture. This produces an overall bleak effect, with a reduction in colour impact.

Blur   A blurred subject can suggest movement, or create an impressionistic

◄ When you include the sun in the frame, the harsh contrasts make exposure control especially tricky. To be sure of at least one good picture, bracket exposures as outlined on page 15.

▲ Restricting the colour palette to a limited range of hues creates subtle pictures that reward a second glance. The sepias that dominate this picture evoke a sense of age – an atmosphere that fits the subject matter perfectly.

effect. If you use a slow shutter speed with a moving subject it will record as a blur in the picture. The slower the speed, the more pronounced the effect. Blurred colour in the subject can stand out against sharp colour background.

Colour match   Try to match your colour film to the subject. A slow film (up to ISO 100) will produce the sharpest and most detailed results. A medium speed film (around ISO 200) is fine for most colour shots, and a faster emulsion (ISO 400 upwards) is needed for low-light colour work. With colour slides make sure you use daylight film for daylight work and a

tungsten-balanced film for working indoors with lamplight.

Colour imbalance   You can deliberately use the wrong type of colour film for effect. Use a daylight-balanced film under lamplight for a warm result in a portrait, for instance. Or use a tungsten-balanced film to make a landscape shot in daylight seem cold and harsh. Or try mixing light sources to wash different parts of the picture with different colours. If you shoot at dusk when light levels indoors and outside are roughly similar, scenes that combine natural and artificial light will be tinged both yellow and blue.

Colour correction   Sometimes colours may not record on film exactly as you see them because of the limitations of the film, so some correction may be needed. Filters can be used to correct colour at the camera stage (see Filter effects page 120) or, with colour negative film, colour correction can be introduced at the printing stage.

Colour effects   Apart from the differing natural effects of colour caused by changeable light, exposure and camera or subject movement, you can introduce colour effects in a number of ways. At the camera stage, special coloured filters can be used to create specific effects. In the darkroom, you can also introduce effects at the printing stage, creating exciting images from quite ordinary negatives or slides (see pages 115-120).

Colour cast   A colour cast or bias in the picture may be an effect of the light – in a snowy landscape, for instance, the light may have a bluish tinge. But if your pictures all have a colour cast, the fault may be on the film itself. The problem may be in the film processing or in the camera. In the first instance check with your processor. If the problem seems to be in the camera, take it and the film back to your camera shop or dealer.

Experiment with exposure to see how it affects colour. On slide film, overexposure turns bright colours to pastel hues.

BLACK-AND-WHITE

Understand black-and-white Black-and-white photography requires a different approach to colour. The colours in the subject are, of course, converted to monochrome so tone, shape and other factors become more important in the final result.

Black-and-white subjects You can shoot practically any subject in black-and-white – but some areas of photography can lend themselves better to monochrome work than others. Popular subjects include landscapes, particularly when there is a strong linear or textural element, portraits, especially elderly faces, and architectural work, where monochrome emphasizes the lines of buildings.

Colour to black-and-white If you are not used to shooting in black-and-white, it may take time to train yourself visually. In a lot of colour work the impact of the subject can rely on the colours. When using black-and-white film look for a good range of tones, interesting shapes, the effect of light, and other factors which will create an interesting effect.

Tonal range Colours reproduce in black-and-white film as a series of tones from black to white, with many shades of grey in between. In a landscape, for instance, colours of trees, land and sky appear as layers of tones. The tonal range varies between subjects – in a shot where similar colours dominate the frame they will reproduce as an overall tone of grey. Look for tonal variety where possible.

High key A lot of bright highlights in the subject will produce a high key effect in a black-and-white shot. Shoot in snow, for instance, and most of the shot will be dominated by a white high-key effect. You can make some shots high key in the darkroom by deliberately under-exposing at the printing stage.

◀ Taking good black-and-white pictures means thinking in terms of tones. Don't make the common mistake of assuming that the picture must contain a full range of tones, with every shade of grey represented. This striking portrait consists only of solid black and clear whites.

▲ Detail is especially important in monochrome, since there are no colours to distract the viewer. When you are trying to highlight texture and pattern, use a slow film to retain more detail, and if possible use a tripod to keep the camera steady.

Pattern and texture Be prepared to work hard at bringing out the pattern and texture in the subject to make it seem 'real' to the viewers. Apart from spotting a good pattern or finding subjects with interesting texture, experiment with shooting and lighting angles for the best effect.

Weather effects Black-and-white results are as dependent on weather variations as colour. If you shoot the same scene in a variety of weather conditions you can see the changes in light direction, general tone and image contrast. Extreme conditions like snow or heat haze, makes a considerable difference to a scene.

Bright light In bright light you can use a fairly small aperture (say, f/16) with a medium speed black-and-white film (around ISO 125) for sharpest results. Watch out for high contrast in bright light; a contrast reducing developer may be needed at the film processing stage.

High-key Similarly light tones dominate high-key pictures. Create them by picking pale subjects, overexposing, and by dodging shadows in the darkroom.

Overcast An overcast sky adds drama to a landscape picture – but it also means you need a longer exposure than would be needed under a clear sky. For a very dark sky where you are not using a fast film you may need a tripod to support the camera while using a slow shutter speed.

Rain and mist If you shoot black-and-white film in heavy rain or mist, remember that there will be a loss of detail, particularly in the distance. Rain has a diffusing effect on light and softens the contrast in a scene. Mist in a landscape can offer an interesting effect but, if you want to reduce the mist for clarity, use a skylight UV filter over the lens.

Avoid grey snow Watch the exposure when photographing snow to avoid the white turning to grey in the final picture. When you take a light reading, deliberately overexpose by half or one f/stop to retain the whiteness. Overexposure will also ensure you retain detail in darker shadow areas.

Low key A low key picture has plenty of dark tones. A landscape shot in an overcast sky, or someone photographed in a dark room, are examples. You can make a picture low key in the darkroom by overexposing at the printing stage to make the picture darker.

Contrast The contrast (the hardness or softness) of a black-and-white picture depends on several factors. Some subjects are more 'contrasty' than others. Also the strength and the direction of light dictates the level of contrast in your negatives, and choose the right paper and developer for increasing or reducing contrast in negatives and prints (see Darkroom chapter, page 112).

Shape and form Without the benefit of colour the shape and form in the subject becomes very important. Outdoors you can find interesting shapes in buildings,

Dye image black-and-white films such as Ilford XP1 are processed in colour negative chemicals. Take them to any colour lab for rapid, inexpensive monochrome prints.

◀ Infrared film captures quite a different range of tones from conventional black-and-white film. For the most dramatic results, fit a visually opaque filter over the camera lens, so that only infrared radiation forms the image.
▼ A red filter used with conventional film darkens the sky and separates out the clouds. Local exposure control when printing provides further opportunities for controlling the shades of grey in the image.

monuments and other architecture, as well as in landscape work. In a portrait the shape of someone's face is as important as expression and lighting.

Wrong film   If you don't have the right film for an assignment, don't worry. You will often be able to achieve an acceptable result by altering the normal processing procedure. If a situation calls for a slow film for maximum detail, but you only have a fast film, *down rate* the film speed by altering the ISO speed from ISO 400 to 200, for instance, and process the film in a fine grain developer at a slightly reduced development time. If you have a slow film for a fast film subject, *uprate* the film and increase the development time.

Film rating   When processing down-rated or uprated film you must make adjustment to development time at the film processing stage. This varies depending on the type of film and developer. Most manufacturers detail the times

needed to develop a particular speed of film in the developer instructions. Read these carefully before proceeding.

Black-and-white filters   You can change the tones in black-and-white pictures by using coloured filters over the camera lens. For example, to bring out cloud detail in a blue sky, use a yellow or orange filter. (See Filters, page 105.)

Overexposure   When you overexpose black-and-white film the negative appears to be dark, particularly in lighter areas of the picture, (white reproduces as black in the negative). Slight overexposure helps retain detail in snow and other situations where lighter tones dominate. If you overexpose you might be able to compensate for this at the film development stage for a more evenly exposed result.

Underexposure   When you under expose a black-and-white film the negative appears to be 'washed out' with little

Dull days make for dull, flat black and white pictures, but you can compensate by increasing development time 25% to add contrast.

detail, particularly in shadow areas. You can create a low key, or dark effect, by deliberately underexposing the film (by one f/stop or more). If the underexposure is accidental, you can correct it by increasing the development time when the film is processed.

Correct film For the best black-and-white results choose the right film for the subject. For most situations choose a medium speed film (ISO 125) but, for more detailed work (close-ups, copying, etc.) a slow film (ISO 50) is best. For fast action and low light photography use a fast film (ISO 400 or faster).

Printing effects You can change the impact of a black-and-white picture in the darkroom. Apart from increasing and reducing the size of the image in the enlarger, you can make the shot seem darker (by over exposing). Using various simple printing tricks you can radically alter how a mono picture looks. (See Darkroom chapter, pages 112-114 for hints on how to do this.)

Composition If you have sufficient detail in the negative, but you are not happy with how the shot has been framed, for a more pleasing result, you can select any area of the negative to print, leaving out any detail not required.

Print trimming and presentation There are several ways of presenting a black-and-white print. First, decide if you want a white border around the edge of the print. Most enlarging masking frames leave a thin border – you can trim this off later if necessary, or print without the frame. Some photographers print on larger sheets of photographic paper, about 38×30 or 51×41cm (15×12 or 20×16in), but print only on a small section, leaving an area of white surrounding the picture, creating more impact.

Black borders Prints that include pale areas can look weak with white borders, because the image fades into border without a definite line between the two. The print will be improved if you rule a black line around the image with Indian ink.

CAMERA EFFECTS

Using blur Set the camera to a slow shutter speed (slower than 1/30 second) for blurred or impressionistic effects that look particularly good in colour. As you press the shutter, quickly draw a circle in the air with the camera lens. With fast moving subjects, you can keep the subject fairly sharp, while transforming the background into a vivid blur, by firing the shutter as you closely follow the movement of the subject with the camera.

Double exposure Superimpose two pictures by using a double exposure technique. Some cameras have a superimpose button – take one shot, press in the button and advance the film wind-on lever to cock the shutter (the film stays where it is for the second exposure). Take a second shot of the subject for a superimposed image. If your camera does not have a superimpose button, press in the rewind button in the base of the camera and hold it in as you wind on (this is possible with 35mm SLR cameras only). For a correct exposure, divide the exposure indicated by the meter by two.

Aperture effect How the aperture is set will affect the depth of field, or region of sharpness in the picture. You can effectively dissolve the background detail by focusing on the foreground and using the widest aperture on the lens.

Masking To make someone appear in the same scene twice, use a mask. Black out half of a circular filter and opaque card and, with the camera on a tripod, expose the left side of the picture with the person in view. Reset the shutter using the superimpose or rewind button, rotate the mask 180 degrees and, with the subject in the right side of the frame, take the second exposure. The result will show the person appearing on both sides of the same shot.

Add the moon to night shots using the double exposure technique described on the right. Use your longest lens to photograph the moon, then turn the camera to photograph the moon-lit landscape with a shorter focal length.

▶ In dim light you may have no choice but to set a slow shutter speed – so why not make virtue out of necessity? Here the blurring caused by setting an exposure of 1/4 second is strongly suggestive of action and exertion.

Slide sandwich You can create unusual effects by sandwiching two different slides in the same mount. Look through your slide collection and combine subjects which differ in size and perspective for best effect. Each slide should be as light as possible otherwise the final sandwich will be too dark. Project the slides together or print them together.

Panoramic views To record a very wide angle of view – when shooting a large expanse of landscape, or a group of people – you can take separate photographs of small sections of the panorama, then stick the prints of each photograph together to make a complete view. You will need to mount the camera on a tripod, point the camera towards one side of the panorama, make an exposure and then swing it round a little to make a second expo-sure . . . and so on until you have taken the complete view.

Mirror image Create an unusual effect by photographing someone's reflection in a mirror, or the subject and the reflection. Some mirrors have natural flaws which can produce slight distortion, or you can use trick mirrors as seen in many fair-grounds. Reflections in other surfaces, like some metallic objects, can also produce odd effects that many people find in-teresting.

Graduated colour A graduated colour filter is half clear, graduating to a deep colour (as in some sunglasses). This can be particularly effective in a landscape, where the land is seen in its normal colour, but the sky takes on the colour of the filter (red, blue, brown, etc.).

▼ Graduated filters tint the sky with colour, or simply darken it to retain more detail. The most useful filters are the subtler ones such as the pale purple used here. Deeper colours look unnaturally bright.

▲ A polarising filter enriches the colour of blue sky, and cuts out reflections from the water's surface. If you rotate the filter in front of your eye, you'll quickly find the orientation that provides maximum effect. With an SLR, fit the filter to the lens, and rotate the filter as you look through the viewfinder.

Zooming   Create streaky lines coming out of the subject by zooming in or out with a zoom lens. With the camera firmly supported (preferably on a tripod) select a reasonably slow shutter speed (1/15 or slower) and move the zoom control during the exposure.

Deeper colour effect   For better colour saturation on sunny days like a deep blue shot for instance, fit a polarising filter. Rotate the filter and watch how the sky appears to deepen in colour, revealing any white cloud detail.

Distortion effect   Any subject can be completely transformed by fitting an ultra wide-angle lens. An 8mm *fish-eye* lens will distort detail giving a 180-degree viewing angle. An *anamorphic* lens attachment can be used to 'squeeze' the image horizontally or vertically for a special effect.

3D effect   To shoot 3D images with your camera, fit a special stereo attachment which records a pair of images on each frame. Use slide film and view the results in a stereo viewer. Alternatively, tape two SLR cameras baseplate to baseplate, make identical exposures of the same subject and view using a stereo slide viewer. Or project the slides using two projectors, fitted with a red and green filter respectively, and provide red and green 3D spectacles for the viewers. The Nimslo 3D camera is a 35mm compact which uses conventional film to produce individual 3D colour prints via a special laboratory process.

Colour spot   A colour spot filter is a one-colour filter with a clear hole in the middle. Keeping the subject in the centre of the viewing area, it will retain its true colour, but be surrounded by the diffused colour of the filter. Try using this filter for portraits, shots of flowers, and so on – but be careful to match the colour of the filter to the subject as carefully as possible.

Strobe effect   If you have the use of a studio and want to capture several repeated images on one frame, use a strobe light. This gives out regular pulses of light and 'freezes' any motion into several overlapping images. For instance, you can capture a tennis player at different stages of a serve, all in one picture. To use strobe, place the subject in front of a black background, open the camera shutter (on the 'B' setting) and start the strobe during the action. Alternatively, fire a flashgun at regular intervals for the same effect.

▼ Caught by a stroboscopic light source, even the common budgie make a fascinating subject. Proper 'strobe' units are costly, but a few of the newer flash units now have a strobe feature that can simulate this effect.

Colour layers You can produce the effect of layers of colour in a picture by fitting a two or three colour filter. This type of filter has two or three different colours, one on top of the other, so that you can produce a sort of colour sandwich. This effect doesn't work well with all subjects and is perhaps most suitable for landscape work. Use it sparingly for good results.

Diffraction There are many filters available which can diffract light for special effect. A 'starburst' filter turns a single bright light source into a star shape – effective in a sunny landscape or with street lamps. Other diffraction filters create a 'rainbow' effect where there are lights in the picture.

Soft focus Introduce a softer effect (in a portrait for instance), by fitting a soft focus filter. You can simulate the effect by smearing Vaseline on a Skylight filter, or shooting through misty glass – keep it close to the lens to avoid reflection.

Multi-image Use a prism filter to make the subject appear several times at once in one shot. When photographing someone with a prism filter, keep the face in the centre of the picture – several faces will then appear around the frame for a multi-image effect. The number of images depends on the number of 'faces' in the prism – you can choose between three or five, sometimes more. Preferably use a three-face prism to avoid a cluttered picture. Always use a simple background to avoid spoiling the effect.

Split lens By fitting a split-lens filter over the lens, you can combine a close-up with a distant view in a way impossible even with the lens set to the smallest aperture. The filter has a semi-circular magnifying lens covering only the bottom half of the picture, which registers the foreground sharply even while the lens is normally focused on the background.

Unusual angle One of the easiest effects to produce is to shoot a familiar subject from an unusual angle. After trying the obvious straight- or side-on approach, try shooting from a high or low angle for effect – you might end up with a better picture as a result.

Coloured light There are plenty of ways you can change the colour of light for special effect. In daylight use coloured filters on the camera. When using flash or lamps cover them with coloured gel filters, adding different colours to the main subject or to the background. Experiment with different colours and see which ones work in particular situations. (See also Filter effects, page 120.)

Back projection You can make your subject appear in practically any location in the world – by projecting a background using a back projection unit. With the subject a few feet away from the projection screen (to avoid casting shadow), you can back project a scene at 45 degrees from the screen. Use tungsten lamps to light the subject so that you can keep a good balance between the lighting and screen brightness, otherwise the illusion won't work. If you don't have access to specialised back projection equipment, try using an ordinary slide projector, and projecting the background onto a white-painted wall or conventional screen. Choose a background slide that does not include regular shapes, as these will be distorted when photographed at an angle.

Beyond the camera Apart from effects created with the camera and accessories, there are plenty of effects which can be created after the pictures have been taken – in the darkroom. There are many printing techniques for both black-and-white and colour which can transform your pictures. See the Darkroom chapter (pages 112-121) for some tips, and look out for advice on darkroom effects in other books and magazines.

Starburst filters don't just add stars to highlights – they blur the picture too. Don't use them when sharpness is critical.

▶ Even for pictures of celebrities and royalty, just being there is never enough – spontaneous, relaxed images demand all the skills of the portrait photographer.

SPECIAL SKILLS

LICHFIELD

Lichfield is one of this country's best-known photographers. A keen amateur since childhood days, he started photographing professionally about twenty years ago. Renowned for his portraits of famous people, including members of the Royal Family, and of beautiful women, his work is stamped by an engaging informality.

Use your imagination Before photographing someone, determine how you want the picture to look. I would try to see the whole thing as a finished shot in my mind – you can even do a rough sketch of what the shot should look like. Decide if the picture is for an album, or a photo frame, and whether it will be portrait-shaped or horizontal. Your initial concept should also take into account clothes, make-up, backgrounds, and so on.

Establish mood Decide on the kind of mood you want to create in the picture. This is determined by the use of either high- or low-key lighting, the choice of background, and the general 'feeling' of the situation. Also decide on the direction in which you are going to shoot. Try to go to the location first to have a look round.

Making the formal informal You can reduce the formality in a portrait by carefully avoiding staid poses and expressions. When you have put someone into a pose, 'rough up' their clothing or hair a bit – they won't look quite so staged. The real secret is to get people to *react* to you. That doesn't mean make them scream with laughter – it's hard to live with a photograph of someone absolutely beaming, but a half-smile will do. You must make them feel they are not just an object you're going to click at. After all, they are the *raison d'être* of the photograph.

Overcoming shyness Choose the time of day when the subject might be most relaxed, with not too many distractions. Don't photograph girls before 11am as their faces take longer to 'wake-up'. Establish a confident rapport – a good chat between the two of you may help. Ask how the person would like to be photographed and perhaps look through a few pictures first. Try to be relaxed yourself. If the photographer is preoccupied with his or her own nerves, there will be little chance of noticing that the person being photographed is probably more nervous.

Where to shoot If you have to decide between shooting someone in the front room or the nearby park, I'm all for going to the park. People react better in a 'natural' situation than in a studio set-up, providing there is some privacy. The front room might be crowded and may have walls which will affect the result if you are using colour. Outdoors, try to use back-lighting: never shoot with the sun behind you, otherwise you get screwed up eyes and shadows on the face.

Timing When shooting anything scenic, always get ready before dawn. With colour film, the low sun will make everything very 'warm', shadows will be blue, and it is generally a good time to shoot. For people who don't want to get up that early, the twilight time in the evening is just as excellent.

◀ Lichfield used a diffusion filter and very soft lighting to soften the laughter lines around the face of 'Housewife Superstar' in this studio shot for LWT. Shot at 1/125 f/16 with a Rolleiflex 6006 and 150mm lens on GPN film.

▲ Low-key lighting and careful choice of props and background gives this portrait of rock star and campaigner Bob Geldof a brooding presence in this studio shot for *TV Times*. Shot at 1/125 f/11 with a Rolleiflex 6006.

► At formal events, it's worth taking a picture without warning, just before everyone thinks you're ready: this way you'll catch relaxed expressions, and not fixed grins. Shot by flash with a Hasselblad with a 150mm lens on EPR120 film.

At weddings (1) For church weddings get everyone outside in a group, preferably somewhere where there are few onlookers. (2) When the bride and groom come out of the church, be ready to photograph there and then. Be careful not to have people in the background when photographing the couple coming out of the church. (3) Talk to the couple beforehand to find out who they want in the groups.

Catch their attention It is important to get everyone looking at the camera at the same time. You can use a whistle for this. One golden rule is to position everyone so they can see the camera – which means the camera can see them. Make some alarming noise to get them all to look at you – the first shot will be one of 'shock-horror', but the second one can record their amusement at their reaction, so be ready for that. If possible, stand on a wall or pair of step ladders and a plank to give you a better vantage point, and also to get their attention.

► Look out for telling backstage scenes at family occasions. Shot with an Olympus OM4 with a 35mm lens on 200 ASA Ektachrome.

Look for candids Keep a second camera, loaded with fast film, for taking candid shots at the church or reception. Often the best pictures are those that are unrehearsed and unplanned. Compact cameras with autofocus and flash are a good choice for this. Try to photograph everyone you can, but be as unobtrusive as possible. Use flash only as a last resort.

People in black-and-white Many photographers believe that black-and-white is the better medium for portraits. Black-and-white requires a slightly different approach to colour. In particular, the infinite variations of tone that make up a portrait in black-and-white depend greatly for their effect on how the subject is lit. You can create subtle or harsh black-and-white portraits, depending on your lighting (and printing) techniques.

Setting up a portrait Try to establish a rapport with your sitter and keep chatting during the session. If your subject appears nervous take a few pictures without any film in the camera – then load up and start shooting when he or she is relaxed.

Expression Try for a range of different expressions – laughing, smiling, frowning, and so on. If the sitter cannot naturally produce a range of expressions, you may have to do some cajoling.

Surroundings You can express a great deal about a person by including their immediate surroundings in the picture. Try this if the subject has a particularly interesting occupation or interest – an artist surrounded by paints and easels, for example. Take the opportunity of involving the sitter in his work or hobby, using the surroundings as a backdrop.

Variety Advanced planning of a portrait session is useful, but don't go in with too many fixed ideas. Allow for some flexibility in your approach to lighting, camera angles, and how you want the subject to look. Vary the backgrounds if possible, and ask the subject to try different clothes, or try changing props.

▼ Actors are advised never to work with animals and children, but for the photographer, pets and infants make valuable allies. They help a subject relax and ignore the camera.

Individual portrait One-to-one portraiture, with photographer and subject facing each other, is the most challenging – and sometimes the most difficult – to tackle. If time isn't a problem take the session at a moderate pace and allow time for yourself and the person being photographed to 'break in'. Good communication will help the results, especially when you want to vary location, lighting or other factors. Take a break if your subject becomes tired or bored – if you need more pictures, start again later.

Couples Two people photographed together can be easier than portraying them individually. Allow the couple to chat between and even during shots to establish a relaxed atmosphere. As well as looking at the camera, they can look at each other for variety. Watch for differences in height, particularly in close-ups; the smaller person can always stand on a box for extra height to 'level out' the portrait – unless, of course, the height difference is part and parcel of the 'flavour' of the portrait.

Small groups Photographing a small group requires some 'people management' on the photographer's part – and a bit of space. Avoid a 'firing line' approach with everyone facing the camera – a slightly side-on profile, with the people less close together, looks more relaxed and maximises space. For unusual shots place individuals in different parts of the picture, and possibly at varying distances from the camera.

Larger groups Don't line up a large group in a straight line – you will either not get them all in or, if you do, their faces will be too small to recognise in the picture. Form them in a semi-circle in front of the camera, in rows if necessary. For formal occasions, like weddings, important people should be at the front, not stuck behind others. Use chairs or raised platforms if needed so that all can be seen.

People at work When you photograph someone at work, follow the person through a range of activity. This might involve a sequence depicting something being made. Lighting in offices, factories and shops can, however, be quite harsh. If there is a lot of fluorescent lighting, you may need to use a colour correction filter (FL-D) for daylight slide film, or use flash.

Babies Most babies are easy to photograph because they are blissfully unaware of the camera. Try to use daylight for indoor shots because flash is likely to frighten a baby. Give your subject a toy to play with; young babies have far livelier

facial expressions when their attention is concentrated on something.

Children Some children are 'naturals' in front of the camera; others are painfully shy. To avoid curious fingers covering your camera, shoot from a discreet distance – a telephoto or zoom lens can be useful for this. Children can produce a wonderful range of expressions, so always be ready to fire quickly. Shy subjects are best photographed at play. The more shy they are, the longer you should allow them to become absorbed by their activity before you start shooting. Again, shoot from a distance with telephoto.

▲ Backlighting suits the soft features of young children – if this group had been posed facing the sun, they would have screwed up their faces against the harsh light. The Walton sextuplets photographed for *Life* magazine at 1/125 f/8 with a Rolleiflex 6006 and 150mm lens on EPN 120 film.

Poses   How you pose your subject can be crucial to the success of a portrait. The person may be more relaxed when sitting directly in front of the camera. Ask if he or she has a 'better' side; and photograph this first to give the person confidence. Try varying the pose so that the subject is looking at the camera from a different direction in each shot.

Character   Some people's faces are full of natural character and can be easy to photograph. Character can be captured in facial expression, movement, and so on. It is often easier to capture someone's character by shooting informally, possibly from a discreet distance using a telephoto or zoom lens.

People in action   If you photograph someone engaged in a particular activity you should still concentrate on facial expression – you are aiming for a portrait, not merely an action shot.

Sequences   Make the most of a portrait session by shooting a sequence of pictures. This sequence can take a particular direction, depending on your requirements. For instance, you can follow a sequence of activity, or ask the subject to try a range of different expressions (happy to sad), or you can simply change the surroundings for each picture. Not all the pictures may work but, with a good choice, you can select the best from the sequence.

Humour   Always be on the lookout for naturally funny situations. It helps if you always carry your camera, so that you can snap amusing situations as they happen. You can find humour at organised events, on the street, or even around the home. Many pictures are funny because they juxtapose separate elements, not amusing in themselves, in a humorous way.

Taking a beauty shot   The first essential ingredient for a successful beauty shot is the right model. An experienced model will be familiar with expressions and poses and may well be able to provide her own make-up and clothes, as well as props, such as jewellery. With an inexperienced model you may need to spend some time beforehand to plan the shot. Try and use diffused or bounced lighting (daylight or flash) and enhance the effect with a soft-focus filter.

Nude photography   It helps if you have worked with a model clothed before asking that person to pose nude. Decide on your approach beforehand and discuss your ideas with the model before you start. Try lighting from different angles to emphasise shape and skin texture. When working in a studio keep it warm for the model's comfort.

Model release   You can acquire full legal rights to the use of your photographs (in publication, for example) by asking your sitter to sign a model release form before you take the pictures. Ask a local modelling agency, or one of the photographic associations for a sample form.

Choosing the best shot   After processing, look carefully through all your pictures and decide on the best ones from the session. With black-and-white, for which you do your own processing, contact all the strips of film onto a single sheet of photographic paper and select the best for enlargement later. Colour enprints can be examined and the best selected for reprinting. Examine slides closely, using a magnifying glass or a projector.

Adding effects   Make your pictures more interesting by adding effects at the darkroom stage. When making a print you can use techniques to alter the impact of the shot (see page 120).

Keeping an album   Store pictures of family and friends in an album. Don't crowd the pages with too many pictures, and vary the sizes of prints.

◀ Studio shot of Jerry Hall for Lichfield's book *The Most Beautiful Women*. Shot by flash at 1/125 f/8 with a Hasselblad and a 150mm lens on black and white TX film.

GEORGE WRIGHT

George Wright took up photography while he was studying graphic design in the early 1970s. His first professional assignments were in fashion photography. During the past decade he has built up impressive portfolios of travel and photo journalism photography in India, the Middle East and the United States. His work appears frequently in the *Observer* and *Sunday Telegraph* magazines.

Preparation Make sure that all your equipment is fully serviceable and comprehensively insured. Too obvious to state perhaps, but mishaps have an uncanny habit of catching all photographers unawares from time to time. A service for well-used camera bodies, a critical eye over scratched filters, sufficient spare batteries for those parts that always run out at the most inconvenient moments, and – if you can afford it – a few more rolls of film than you reckon on shooting: all these are wise precautions and can help prevent disappointment after you return home.

Research Find out as much as you can about where you are going *before* you get there. Check with travel agents and tourist boards for the times and dates of any special events. Plan a photographic itinerary of possibilities. Read about and look at pictures of the place, and, most importantly, buy maps and study them. If it is going to be hot, remember that you are going to have to keep your film cool at all times (never leave it in the boot of a car left in the sun). Sand in the form of desert or beach requires extra thought in the camera-cleaning department.

Travelling However you are travelling, give extra thought to how you pack your camera bag. Know where each item is and always keep a loaded camera ready for recording your journey. If you are going abroad ensure that you know the requirements for customs clearance. Carry a typed list, in duplicate (leave one copy at home), of your numbered equipment. Customs are not usually a problem for most people on holiday, but restrictions vary from country to country and it is always best to check them out first. If you are flying, carry your gear in a case or bag that conforms with hand-luggage requirements.

Arriving Resist the temptation to rush out on the first day and shoot too much film. Always carry your camera, but try and decide what it is about the place that draws you while being ready to get the picture that you might never see again. It is always worth looking at local postcards; they can be extremely informative, if only in showing you what to avoid. Keep a notebook so that you can caption your pictures with the relevant details.

Shops and markets These are good places to photograph everyday local life. Spend some time looking around a market and you will come up with that universal image of commerce with its own particular local flavour. An overcast day is usually an advantage, as harsh sunlight and hard shadows will cause problems of excessive contrast. Look for details, signs and shop fronts as well as the general activity. Piles of produce make good still life subjects, but always ask permission to photograph inside a shop. And always be ready to shoot inside the bar!

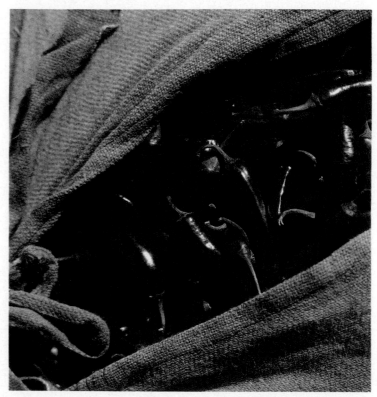

◀ The Taj Mahal taken from a window of the nearby Red Fort. Shot at 1/30 f/16 with a polarising filter and 28mm lens on Kodachrome 64.
▼ Detail from the vegetable market at Cavaillon, France. Shot at 1/125 f/8 with a 105mm lens on Kodachrome 64.

▲ A reflected image of the Coliseum in Rome. Shot at 1/125 f/16 with a 105mm lens on Kodachrome 64.
► The Campo de Fiori market, Rome, shot at 1/60 f/11 with a 25mm lens on Kodachrome 64.

People   They make the place what it is, and you are probably going to want to photograph them. Observe local customs (in some parts of the world being photographed is considered a grave infringement on personal privacy) and, when appropriate, ask permission. This may well get you invited into a part of life that most tourists miss. A Polaroid camera for giveaway pictures is often a rewarding thing to carry, as the unwilling can often be softened with the promise of an instant photograph to take home.

In the city   A map of the city centre and a good pair of shoes are indispensable. It may be worthwhile to go on a sightseeing bus tour; at least it will give you a convenient if predictable view of the obvious sights. Take your family or friends on the conducted tour so that you can feel justified in returning at a later date on your own. Find a tall building with public access to photograph the city from a high viewpoint; the tourist-information office will usually be able to help you here. Night shots – especially after rain, when the pavements reflect the neon lights – are worth considering, so you will need to carry a tripod for long exposures. Some museums allow visitors to take photographs as long as no flash or tripods are used, so you may want to carry some fast film for such occasions.

Tourist sites   Do not discount the obvious: it does not matter how many times a famous place has been photographed, there is always a different way of looking at it. After all, it would be a singular photographer who visited Agra and declined to take pictures of the Taj Mahal simply because it is the most photographed object in Asia. Go there at less-popular times of day; at dawn for instance, when the other tourists are still in bed. Look for new angles, odd juxtapositions or reflections. With imagination, a national monument that has become a holiday-snap cliché may well be photographed in an original way.

Events and carnivals   These always provide strong, colourful pictures. The participants in a carnival will not object to being photographed; they expect it and invariably play up to the camera. The problems encountered when photographing such events will more likely be to do with finding the best place in the crowd, so arrive before the action starts. This will give you the chance to select the best viewpoints before everyone else gets there, and also provide the opportunity to record the preparations and behind-the-scenes activity.

Where to go   Choose somewhere that will inspire you to take good photographs. Countries with interesting scenery, architecture and local costumes offer great scope for photography. The mountains and lakes of Scotland or the Alps may appeal, or the ornate buildings of Amsterdam, or the bridges of Venice. Also consider the likely seasonal weather.

What to take   Take only what you plan to use. A simple automatic compact camera is sufficient for holiday snaps, but for greater flexibility take a 35mm SLR camera with three lenses – a 28mm wide-angle, 50mm standard and 100mm or 135mm telephoto. A ×2 teleconverter will extend your lens range still further.

Protect your lenses with skylight filter. Two camera bodies enable you to shoot scenes in both black-and-white and colour at the same time. Take more film than you think you will need – it may be difficult to obtain, or more expensive abroad. Include a flashgun with spare batteries. Use a lens hood to reduce flare and to protect your lenses.

Instant pictures   Producing a picture 'on the spot' can be a great advantage. You can give an instant snapshot of a subject to someone who has helped you set up the picture, while you can take other shots with your SLR camera. An instant camera can also be used when quality is not a top priority. With this type of camera you are more likely to take pictures on occasions when you might not have bothered with your SLR.

Carrying your gear   Take a soft camera bag as hand luggage on a plane and stow it under the seat. Most bags have padded partitions to separate lenses and cameras. A robust aluminium case with foam padding inside offers greater protection. The case can also be used as a seat or to stand on in order to see over a crowd of people. Aluminium reflects the sun and keeps film and cameras cooler. But a hard case is not as easy as a soft shoulder bag to dip into when you want to change film or lenses.

Cameras for the sea   Most cameras are badly affected by sea water; the water wrecks film and electrics and salt corrodes the body. But you can shoot pictures near or in the sea with a waterproof 110 or 35mm compact camera. These are not true underwater cameras, however – unlike the 35mm Nikonos which has interchangeable lenses and a built-in light meter, but it requires a separate underwater flash. It can be used to a depth of 50 metres (165ft). You can get an underwater housing for your conventional camera; or you can use a plastic inflatable bag with a clear 'porthole' in shallow water.

Additional pouches Put each lens into an individual pouch in the camera bag to give it more protection. If you are planning to be very active, do away with a large camera bag and use a purpose-made bag or pouch which threads onto a belt, harness, or straps; some of these pouches are waterproof. This will leave your hands free to operate your camera.

Insurance Consider insuring all of your photographic equipment. Don't assume that it is included in a policy which covers personal effects: read the small print, and note the exclusions. Some policies may cover your gear worldwide, *but not in transit*. Others do not pay out if you lose or damage a camera while taking part in a 'risk' sport, such as scubadiving or mountain climbing.

Expect the unexpected Always be ready to take a picture. Know where your camera is, have a place for each item of equipment and return it there after use. Make sure the camera is always loaded and there are several frames left on the roll. Learn to operate the controls quickly. Pre-set the aperture and shutter speed for an average exposure – perhaps 1/125 sec at f/8 with medium-speed film.

Photographs from the air Try to get a window seat on a plane, in front of the wing. Clean off any bits of dirt on the inside of the window. Don't worry too much about odd scratches since they will be out of focus and hardly discernible in the photograph. Set the focus at infinity and hold the camera close to the window. Avoid taking pictures looking obliquely through the perspex window, as this usually gives a blurred image. An ideal time for taking pictures is when the aircraft is banking in a turn, so that you have a clear view of the ground beneath.

▶ Picture of Bath taken from a hot air balloon at 1/60 f/16 with a 20mm lens on Kodachrome 64.

Choice Choose what interests you. Monuments, landscape, moody shots, local people, members of your own travel group or whatever – but don't restrict yourself to obvious subjects. Look for detail in local craftwork, or focus on just one aspect of a building, or a close-up of someone. These details often say more about a community than an overall view.

Tell a story Build up an overall picture of your trip through sequences of photographs. Depict where you are staying, what the scenery is like, how the locals dress, and so on. Include pictures of daily activity whether that is simply people lying on the beach or doing something more imaginative. Record people at work – mending nets, working in the fields, or selling vegetables. A coherent view of your trip will be more interesting and rewarding than a set of unrelated pictures.

Which lens? Use medium telephoto lens (100mm or 135mm) to photograph people without getting under their feet. This lens is also ideal for portraits. The small depth of field makes the subject stand out because the background is thrown out of focus. This length of lens also flattens, rather than exaggerates, facial features. A wide-angle lens (28mm or 35mm) can add drama to a picture: anything close will be exaggerated.

Keep on clicking Film is much cheaper than the cost of your trip, so don't be miserly with it. When you see an interesting subject don't just take one picture – keep on clicking. People can often be very self-conscious at first. Once you have taken a photo they relax – that's when you should take more shots. Use a motordrive or autowinder to shoot fast sequences and not miss anything.

▲ Balloons provide a convenient and relatively stable platform for photography, and allow you to approach a subject more closely than would be safe in a light aircraft. Trees shot at 1/60 f/11 with a 24mm lens on Kodachrome 64.

People and backgrounds Avoid confusing backgrounds. If you want the viewer's attention to be focused on one person or a group of people, separate them from their surroundings. You can do this either by using a telephoto lens to put the background out of focus, by positioning the people in front of a plain wall or hedge, or by crouching down so there is mostly sky behind them. Always bear in mind that, by including *some* of the background detail, you will help give the picture a sense of place; but this should not detract from the main subject of your photograph.

Landscape angle To avoid a 'flat' travel picture, have a person, river or road leading into a landscape to give it depth. To emphasise an interesting foreground use a wide angle lens and shoot from a low vantage point. Or, if you want to avoid an unsightly foreground, a telephoto lens will allow you to be selective about what you include. Guidelines such as 'Don't place the horizon across the middle of the frame' and 'Don't put the main subject in the centre of the picture' are only guidelines, *not* laws. It is best to experiment so you trust your judgment.

Framing A natural frame helps focus attention and lead the eye into the picture. An obvious choice is to use a tree, window or archway. Also look for more unusual 'frames' – your subject could be framed by the design painted on a famous building, or by a waterfall. But don't let the frame overpower the main subject.

Atmosphere Whatever the weather, keep your camera handy. Don't put it away just because the sun goes in. Interesting 'atmosphere' photographs can be taken in a tropical rainstorm, but shoot from shelter to keep your camera as dry as possible. Ominous storm clouds can turn a mundane looking landscape into a dramatic scene. Look out for a rainbow as the storm clears.

Lighting shift Throughout the day the light shifts. Be prepared to return to a scene at a time when the sun is lighting it most effectively. The low angle of the sun in the early morning and just before sunset generally gives the best results. This light is more flattering to both landscapes and people than the harsh mid-day sun. In the mountains, the early morning sun often glows pink on the snow for a few minutes. Be ready for it. And watch for shafts of sunlight shining through trees or windows.

Sunsets If you include the sun in the viewfinder frame, the intense light will give a very high meter reading, which would result in a very dark result. Over-expose the shot by one or two f/stops to record some detail in the sky and the landscape. Bracket your exposures to strengthen or weaken the colours. In the tropics the sun sets faster than in temperate latitudes, so you have to act quickly.

Night scenes Some of the best travel shots can be taken at night, particularly in bright neon-lit cities. Use a long exposure to record night time scenes successfully, as long as there is *some* light. Look for general street scenes, but look also for more close-up detail. Many cities have open street markets at night, selling food, trinkets, and so on. Always take your camera along – flash helps for poor light situations; or use a fast film (ISO 400 or faster) for candid shots.

By the sea Cameras can tolerate a certain amount of freshwater, but salt water is a killer and must be avoided. Wipe affected cameras with a lint cloth lightly soaked in WD40 or similar light oil. If you take a camera on a sandy beach, first grease the joints, mounts and hinges. Then tape over parts not in use, such as the sync socket, motordrive terminal, and so on. Protect the camera in a bag. When changing films find a sheltered, shady spot. Store everything in plastic bags.

Hot climates If a camera is left in very hot direct sunlight, the glue holding the lens elements in place can melt. When you pick up the camera, the elements may be knocked out of place. If possible, store film in a fridge and remove it at least two hours before loading it into the camera. Insulating bags are available, into which you place freezer sachets to keep film and cameras cool. At the end of each day clean your equipment with a soft brush or cloth to remove sand and dust.

Cold climates If you are venturing into extremely cold environments, with temperatures below −32°C (−25°F), the first problem you will encounter is probably battery failure. Even in the conditions you can meet on a skiing holiday, the batteries in an SLR may only last 45 minutes or so. So always take spare batteries, kept in a warm pocket. When returning to a warm room keep the camera in an airtight bag with silica gel packets to reduce condensation.

Look after yourself *You* are the one who takes pictures. In hot climates, drink plenty of water, keep out of direct sunlight except for short periods and wear a hat and loose clothing. In cold climates dress accordingly – if you allow the core of your body to get cold, you will suffer from exposure and be out of action for several days. Avoid touching the frozen metal parts of the camera as bare skin will stick to them.

Buying film abroad Most countries in the western world have supplies of the most popular film types, but the film is often more expensive. If you use an unusual film, or are travelling to a remote area, it is safer and cheaper to take with you more film than you expect to use. Buying a film type you are not used to may produce disappointing results. If a small shop in an out-of-the-way village happens to stock the type of film you want, check the expiry date on the pack as the turnover of stock is probably very slow.

▲ Italian townscape taken at 1/30 f/16 with a 70-200 zoom lens, tripod and cable release on Kodachrome 64.

EAMONN MCCABE

Eamonn McCabe works for the *Observer* newspaper, covering every kind of
sporting event from all-in wrestling to croquet. He has a stylish, often humorous
approach to sports work, as well as an unerring ability to capture the essence of
a sporting occasion. In 1984, not for the first time, he was voted Sports
Photographer of the Year.

Freezing the action Use the highest shutter speed you can: it's better to use 1/500sec at f/2.8 than 1/250sec at f/4. The extra f-stop will not help to sharpen an out-of-focus photograph but the extra speed might help freeze the action. Action going across your field of view needs higher shutter speeds than action coming towards you.

Backgrounds In many ways the most important tip in sports photography is to make sure the background is as clear as possible. There is nothing worse than having a good photograph of, say, rugby or basketball, in which there is a tree or a concrete post coming out of somebody's head in the background. Avoid distracting signs and advertising boards. Try to get a plain background that will allow the viewer to concentrate on the action.

Peak of the action Most sports have moments in them when the players reach a peak of effort which makes for good photographs. A basketball player leaping to score, a boxer landing a knockout punch, a long jumper at the highest point over a sandpit. In football, never follow the ball but aim the camera where you expect the ball to drop. This will give you more time to focus and choose the right moment to shoot your picture.

Be aware Look for photographs as soon as you get to an event or training session. Players preparing, tense faces, managers giving orders, warm-up routines: such pictures often say more about a sport than an action photograph taken during the event itself. Also, pictures of joy or distress after a match or race can tell a great deal about a sport

Length of lens Most amateur photographers' first attempts at sports photography suffer from the photographer not using a long enough lens. When starting out, a good rule is to use a longer lens than you first thought of for a particular shot.

This has the effect of increasing the size of the image on the negative, which will give you more drama.

Film speed Sports photographers increase the speed of the film they are using in order to obtain usable negatives or transparencies from bad-light situations – such as floodlight football and boxing matches. A black-and-white film of ISO 400 can be pushed in processing to ISO 1600 without too much loss in quality. By so doing, the photographer will gain two stops and can shoot at 1/250sec at f/2.8 instead of 1/60sec at f/2.8. This will help freeze the action – whereas a setting of 1/60sec could result in a blur and give an unusable result. Modern colour films can be uprated with very pleasing results.

Panning The trick with this technique is to pre-focus on a spot where you think your subject – a runner, racing car, horse or whatever – will pass: and to use a slow shutter speed to shoot as you follow the action through the spot where you have focused. Fire the shutter as the subject passes the point of focus. Remember to follow the subject smoothly all the way as it goes past you, and not to stop when you let the shutter go.

Zoom lens When shooting a sport such as rugby or horse racing, if you quickly zoom the lens in or out during exposure, the subject in the centre can be reasonably sharp while everything else is a blur. You can thus create an impression of rapid movement.

Silhouettes By underexposing a group of runners or race horses and taking your light reading from the sky in the background, you can achieve a very striking photograph which concentrates on the silhouettes of the runners or horses against the sky rather than on expressions and effort. A yellow or red filter will increase the contrast between subject and background to give a very punchy result.

◀ Female hurdlers shot at Crystal Palace at 1/1000 f/5.6 with a 300mm 2.8 lens on TRI X film.

Knowing the sport The best sports to photograph in the beginning are the ones you know best. If you have a pretty good idea of what's going to happen next it gives you much more time to set yourself up for really effective action shots.

People in sport Sport is all about people. It's the people who drive racing cars, sit on the horses, and pedal the bicycles. Be alert to any development that may arise out of this, whether it's a head-to-head confrontation at a tennis match, or the grimly determined faces of the leading bunch in a marathon race. A violent tackle in a football match may lead to a sudden flare-up between the players. Be prepared to home in quickly on this.

Be prepared Before an action shot, do your homework. Check out locations, consider the best shooting positions. Check the weather and take enough film of the correct speed. For football pictures find out which is the stronger team – and head for the opposition's goal. Consider the lighting – try, for simplicity, to keep the sun behind the shoulders.

Be flexible However thorough your preparation, don't fall into the trap of thinking your photographic assignment will go like clockwork. During any sports event, there are so many possible incidents and developments that the photographer with a too rigid approach will miss the best shots. Be ready for controversy, look for the inevitable elation and dejection – there may be the chance of a good shot of the crowd or the team manager. Always be prepared for the unexpected.

Winners Look for winning shots: the footballer in the act of scoring, the athlete breasting the finishing tape, the tennis player leaping the net, etc. Use a long lens to move in close and tight – it's the facial expression that can make or break a picture. Even down at the local park the expression of a winner can be just as interesting as that of a superstar.

Losers For every winner there are a hundred losers. Discretion is very important. It's an unwise photographer who goes too close to a sore, tensed-up, frustrated sportsman. Try to place the loser in the context of his particular sport. A tennis player who has lost is, for a very short while, isolated in his half of the court; try to portray that sense of isolation and despair.

Spectators Every major sporting event can attract its own particular type of spectators – the hat brigade at Ascot, strawberries and cream eaters at Wimbledon, football supporters at an international match, etc. The techniques are simple – keep an eye open for the characters in the crowd who typify the event, and go for a picture sequence to recreate the scene.

The start The peak of the action shots isn't always at the finish – the start can sometimes offer more. For a horse race or athletics sprint, look for pent-up energy on the competitors' faces. In a race let the starting gun fire and the athletes start to move out of their blocks before exposing.

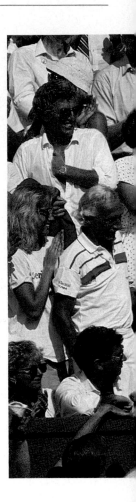

▼ Ladies Day at Ascot. Shot at 1/500 f/8 with a Nikon 500mm f/8 mirror lens on TRI X 400 ASA.

The finish Shooting the finish of an athletics race is all about timing and anticipation. At the precise moment when the winner crosses the line, he is likely to hold his arms aloft in victory. To record this successfully, pre-focus on the finish line and anticipate the exact moment when the victor crosses it. Wait too long and the shot can be missed.

Sprints The finish of a sprint race is particularly difficult because the competitors are in lanes. Unless there is a dead cert, the winner could emerge from any one of eight lanes. The best choice is a lens that isolates two or three runners. Keep an eye on the race to see which one is likeliest to win and concentrate on him or her.

Midway As well as the start and finish, the middle of a race can provide top shots. A group of middle distance runners bunched together, jostling in a pack, works extremely well through a long lens which compresses them together as they approach the camera.

Eye level By far the most comfortable positions for shooting sport are standing and crouching/sitting. A camera case is very useful for support. You can sit on it – handy on a wet day – and, if you want a bit of extra height, it's ideal for standing on. Crouching down slightly and shooting up towards the sportsmen is a simple way to emphasise action. A slightly high angle can portray the players against their pitch or court.

▲ This image, taken moments after Pat Cash won the Wimbledon final, would lose much of its impact if the crowd was cropped out. Shot at 1/1000 f/5.6 with a 400mm f/3.5 lens on Fuji 100 ASA film.

Worm's-eye view Adopt a very low viewpoint for an unusual angle. This often has to be deliberately set up, but that needn't detract from the action. A gymnast in a graceful pose, shot from a low angle, gives a dramatic effect. For this type of shot, a wide-angle lens is required. Avoid one that is too wide as this would distort the subject; a 35mm lens is ideal.

Bird's-eye view At the other extreme, a picture taken looking down onto the subject is effective. In a basket sport, such as netball, you might be able to set up a shot by climbing up the pole and shooting through the net at the players below. Court markings, as in netball, tennis, badminton, and so on, can add an attractive background pattern to overhead shots.

Fast frame For professionals, a fully fledged motor-drive is standard equipment, giving automatic film advance at five frames per second (fps). There are slightly slower models at three-and-a-half frames, and also highly specialised ones giving 12 and even 14fps. Most recent SLRs and many 35mm compact also have motorized film-winding, although they tend to be slightly slower than the average pro motor-drive. If you use the 'single frame' advance mode on the winder, film is wound on automatically, but you must press the shutter button for the next frame. With the winder set for continuous advance, the shutter fires automatically each time. Set for single-frame control: it allows you to fire exactly when *you* want to.

Sequences With a motorized film wind, you can shoot continuous sequences. A set of five or six pictures in a row can tell a story that a single shot can't. With a motordrive a 6sec sequence will produce 30 pictures, so use a 36 exposure film. Follow important action but don't get carried away, otherwise you will have a lot of wasted film.

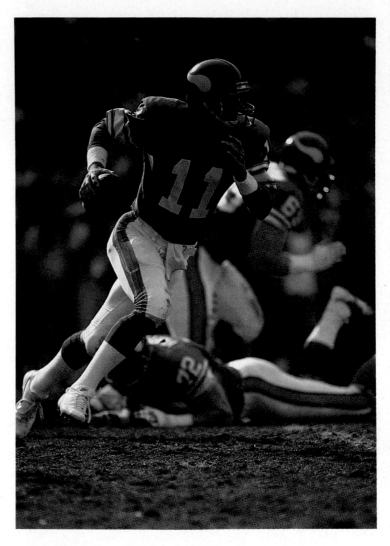

Indoor sports Shooting indoors presents a few specific problems. With relatively low light levels, requiring slow shutter speeds, it makes sense to use flash. But, more often than not, flash is banned at indoor sports events because it can distract competitors. Check beforehand whether you can use flash.

Daylight or tungsten film? Outdoor floodlit events present a problem. At these the subjects are usually too far away for flash to be effective. In these cases, fast film must be used. But you have to decide

▲ Wade Wilson, Minnesota Vikings quarterback, shot at 1/1000 f/5.6 with a 400mm f/3.5 lens on Fuji 100 ASA.

between daylight and tungsten film with colour.

Before the sports event, try to find out what the lighting is; but be warned – there are even different qualities of floodlighting. If in doubt, it's probably best to opt for daylight film which gives a warm cast – more pleasing than the cold tungsten effect.

Black-and-white or colour? Choosing between black-and-white and colour largely depends on personal preference and/or the final use of your pictures. Black-and-white is ideal for the photographer with a darkroom and who may want to sell prints to the people being photographed or to newspapers or magazines. Colour prints are fine for showing around to friends. Colour slides can be projected or submitted to magazines for publication. Choose colour to show the brightly coloured competitors in action.

Fast or slow? Although fast film is usually best for action, don't overlook the possibility of using slow films when the light is bright. In shots taken on a good day, the graininess of fast film can be really obtrusive – especially in the sky. Providing the light is strong enough to allow a fast shutter speed, you may be able to use a slowish film (between ISO 50 and 100) for top quality results.

All-rounder The best all-round film choice is ISO 200. This combines fine grain with a certain amount of speed. It is very useful for sports and action since spending the whole day outdoors might easily involve several changes in the weather. ISO 400 films are faster, but grain is more apparent. They come into their own on a typical, overcast winter day where fast shutter speeds are essential.

Floodlights When shooting under floodlights, films faster than ISO 400 are necessary. There are a range of ultra-fast films generally available, which will all give pretty good results in low light. If the light does get too low, try some creative shots using very slow shutter speeds for effect. The consequent blur of colour can be quite artistic – and it can certainly suggest energetic action.

LOCATIONS

All at sea Yachting, windsurfing and offshore powerboat racing all present one major problem – the action is usually too far away from the shore-based photographer. The best solution is to beg a ride on another boat to get in close. Don't get in the way of the competitors, hold the camera rock steady to negate the boat's motion, and take meter readings especially carefully – bright sky and sea can fool the camera meter.

Shoot wide Moving in close gives excellent shots of yachts. The billowing of the sail is exaggerated, creating a larger-than-life effect. At the other extreme, a row of masts taken through a long tele lens can be equally effective. Shots from the racing yacht itself are dynamic. The crew, busy in action, the surf pounding over the decks, a picture with part of the yacht in the foreground, are possibilities.

In the swim Swimming events usually take place in the calmer waters of a pool. Usually the key swimmers are in the centre lanes, requiring a 300mm tele to close in on the head and shoulders. Front crawl and backstroke are best taken from the side – make sure the swimmer turns his head towards the camera – while breast stroke and butterfly should be captured from the end, with the swimmer coming towards the camera. Remember to vary the approach and angle.

Diving in The start of a swimming race provides excellent opportunities. Shoot for a position slightly higher than the swimmer, and stand on a spot equivalent to a couple of metres into the first length.

When the starter's gun fires, capture the swimmers in full extension as they reach for the water. A shutter speed of at least 1/500sec is needed. A shorter lens will capture all eight swimmers; a longer one isolates just a few, to give an unusual shot.

Below the water line Synchroswimming provides the photographer with line and form in a graceful manner. A pair of smiling faces, with arms outstretched harmoniously, makes good material. But a more eyecatching view can be obtained from below the water line. Many pools have portholes for this, offering a fish's view of the proceedings. The portholes can also be used for shooting racing swimmers. The view from below can reveal much about swimming techniques.

Follow the action Many sports make photography easy because they take place in an arena. For marathons or similar long distance events be prepared to move with the action. Ride on the back of a friend's motorcycle for best shots.

On the road To get the best shots, go over the route yourself beforehand and select two or three vantage points. For a popular event, you will need to get to the best positions early. Try to get a shot, possibly looking downhill, which will allow the race leaders to be contrasted with the rest of the field further down the road. Once the field has gone past, it will be difficult to overtake them for another shot.

Marathons Shooting the big-city marathon races presents problems. With several thousand runners, it is impossible to photograph them more than once together unless they are running several laps of a set course. Aim for interesting faces among the runners, particularly towards the end – the pain will be showing. In large towns, setting the runners against a famous building or bridge gives good perspective.

Silence For sports where silence is required of onlookers, you are up against it. That's why pictures of snooker players in competitive action are few and far between. It's a similar story with golf, although less extreme. On the tee or the putting green, the last thing a golfer wants is the click and whirr of a camera to distract him from his shot. You can't position yourself at a distance and use a tele lens – the crowds around the green would obscure your view. Take the picture just *after* the golfer has hit the ball.

Climb every mountain Good shots of rock climbers and mountaineers owe as much to physical fitness and skill as they do to photographic technique. Dispense with the camera bag – a back-pack is better, with copious pockets to hold equipment, and is essential if you, too, have to use a rope. Lightweight equipment is also better; a zoom lens is preferable to several different lenses, especially if you want to change focal length quickly.

Reflection Snowy mountain tops and ski-ing shots present problems with metering. The dazzling snow, especially on sunny days, fools the camera meter to give an under-exposed result. Most automatic cameras have a manual override facility, and many have an exposure lock. With either, you can find roughly the right exposure for the scene by pointing the camera at the palm of your hand to take an exposure reading or set the exposure lock. With portraits, meter the subject's face if you can.

Haze Shooting high up in the mountains and by the sea can give a problem with ultraviolet haze, which is recorded on film like a blue mist. The problem is reduced by using a skylight UV filter on the front of the lens.

Freeze action With sports and other action shots, use a fast shutter speed to stop the movement. Some SLR cameras have a maximum shutter speed of 1/4000sec, but 1/1000sec is sufficient when shooting sideways at the action. If the action is head on, then 1/500sec or even 1/250sec will do.

Pan with action The problem with freezing the action using high shutter speeds is that the sense of movement is lost. A racing car, pin sharp against a sharp background, might just as well have been parked at the track-side – even though it may have been travelling at 150mph! So, when shooting from the side, track the subject with the camera, and use a relatively slow shutter speed (1/125sec) to record a sharp subject, with the background appearing as a mass of streaks.

Slow speeds for creativity Don't discount slow speeds for good action shots. Panning the action at very slow speeds creates off-beat effects. Athletes running round a track can be panned at 1/15sec or slower, at which speed their upper bodies

will be recorded sharply while their legs will show a lot of movement and given an impression of speed. If you combine panning with zooming – the end result might not look much like sport – but it may be interestingly impressionistic.

Squeeze, don't jerk When shooting action photography, whether a fast or slow speed is used, try to keep the camera as steady as possible. Practise firing the shutter correctly – it can make the difference between a dramatic picture and the one that got away. Squeeze the shutter release and feel for the precise moment when it goes off. Repeat the action time and again until it becomes second nature – a fraction of a second can make all the difference in action photography.

Isolating detail When using a particular lens, aim to isolate signficant detail. To avoid acres of wasted space in the picture, highlight the peak of the action. For these shots, a long lens is usually required.

◄ Close-up of Sylvester Mittee, shot at 1/250 f/5.6 with a 180mm f/2.8 lens on TRI X 400 ASA.

Steady does it When following high-speed action with long lenses, you must hold the camera steady. A tripod isn't much use because it is too cumbersome. A monopod (a one-legged support) is useful with long and heavy lenses and gives freedom of movement. Or you can use a rifle grip, which allows a degree of shoulder support. Otherwise, pull your elbows into the body, grip the lens tightly in one hand and the camera firmly in the other for support.

Longer than long Some sports must be tackled with extremely long lenses. Cricket is typical – with all the action in a small strip in the centre of the arena, you may find that the 'standard' lens needs to be nothing less than a 600mm telephoto. Shooting from the stands at a football match or an athletics meeting requires a lens of similar focal length. If you have only a short lens, shoot a wider expanse of the field, or wait until the action gets closer to your position.

Doubling up Use a 2× teleconverter to 'double up' the focal length of your lens: making an 80mm lens a 160mm, for instance. The problem with converters is the loss of light. While a 2× converter doubles focal length, it also lessens the amount of light reaching the film by the equivalent of two f/stops. Many professionals use a 1.4× converter, which makes a 600mm lens into an 840mm; the light loss with this is only 1 to 1½ f/stops.

Inexpensive telephotos Medium telephoto lenses range from 200 to 400mm. More importantly, they don't cost the earth. They are most useful when you can't get close to the action. To concentrate on football mid-field action, using a 300mm lens will allow you to follow the action and fill the frame satisfactorily. In athletics, the shot-putter doesn't want to be disturbed by the click of a shutter at a crucial moment: a 200mm lens will allow you to take the shot out of earshot.

Short stretch Lenses of 100 to 135mm are very useful – and don't overlook these settings if your zoom is 80-200mm. At a football match, this sort of length is ideal for goal-mouth action, allowing you to include strikers, goalkeeper and the goal without taking in the whole of the main stand as well. At many sports events it is possible to get close to the action, negating the need for a long lens.

Long but portable Mirror lenses are a cheap and portable alternative to telephotos. With a fixed aperture (usually f/5.6 for 300mm and f/8 for 500mm) they range from 300mm to 600mm or even 1000mm. The 300mm is only slightly longer than the typical 50mm standard lens and is easy to use. Taking up minimal space in the gadget bag, it is very useful at a sports event where a lot of walking is involved, and where tele lenses can become very tiring to use.

Wide impact Fit a wide-angle lens to create greater impact. Provided the action becomes very close you can emphasise the dramatic perspective a wide-angle creates. Wide-angle lenses distort the image elongating those subjects towards the edges of the frame. In motorcycle scrambling and motorcross, for instance, where motorbikes fly through the air, careful positioning can ensure that the front wheel is toward the edge of the frame for best visual impact.

Ultra-wide effect There are occasions when a fish-eye lens or an ultra-wide-angle can be used to great effect. The pole vault is a difficult subject to capture on film. One way is to use a fish-eye lens, with its semi-circular view, from directly beneath the bar. From here you can include the landing mat, bar supports – and the vaulter right at the top. These specialised lenses can be used with great effect for one-off pictures; it's up to the photographer to visualise specific shots to get the most from them.

◄ Stopping action like this means using a very fast shutter, and the widest aperture on your lens. This results in very shallow depth of field, so accurate focusing is essential. Shot at 1/1000 f/5.6 with a Nikon 400mm f/3.5 lens on TRI X 400 ASA.

HEATHER ANGEL

Heather Angel trained as a zoologist, and worked as a marine biologist, then took up wildlife photography and became President of The Royal Photographic Society from 1984-86. She has travelled all over the world – including five visits to China – in search of plants and animals to photograph. She is a prolific author, having written 38 books on photography, natural history and gardening.

Appraise the background When taking any pictures of plants, but especially close-ups, always look carefully at the background. Does it conflict with the foreground interest? Check that there are no unsightly vapour trails in the sky, hosepipes on a lawn, or rubbish in the background. A perfect bloom can be ruined by a tatty dead seed-head behind it, or even an out-of-focus blob of bright colour. Often only a small change of the camera angle is what's needed to get a slightly different but greatly improved background.

Creating depth A clump of flowers, a gate or an archway not only helps to provide foreground interest to a picture, but also invites the eye into the picture. Remember you see vistas in three dimensions, but a photograph is a two-dimensional image. Look carefully at the direction of the light, which can also help to create depth by casting strong shadows.

A high viewpoint Look for a seat, a low wall or the top of a shed to gain an elevated view of a garden. A view from just a few feet above normal eye-level will provide a better perspective of a garden layout, while a first-floor window of a house overlooking a garden will give the next best thing to a bird's-eye view. A hill or a cliff top can offer a high-level, and perhaps dramatic, view onto a stream, a lake or a coast line.

A low viewpoint Try crouching down to get a low-angle view of a large, tall flower or a spray of flowers or leaves against the sky. This will provide an uncluttered background which allows all attention to be focused on the subject itself. Statues can also be photographed in this way, with sky as backdrop.

Reflections in water Still water in a pond or lake reflects its surroundings like a mirror. Look for waterside trees, shrubs, 'temples', statues or birds, which repeat themselves as upside-down images in calm water. A perfect reflection, however, is quickly destroyed by wind blowing across water or by a rising fish sending ripples across the surface.

▼ Grey heron standing on a bank of the Thames. Taken at dawn from a boat using a 300mm lens on a Nikon F3 using Ektachrome 200.

▶ Studio shot of Costa Rican flying frog on a vertical sheet of glass to simulate flying in mid-air. A single flash was used, on a Hasselblad with an 80mm lens on Professional Ektachrome 64.

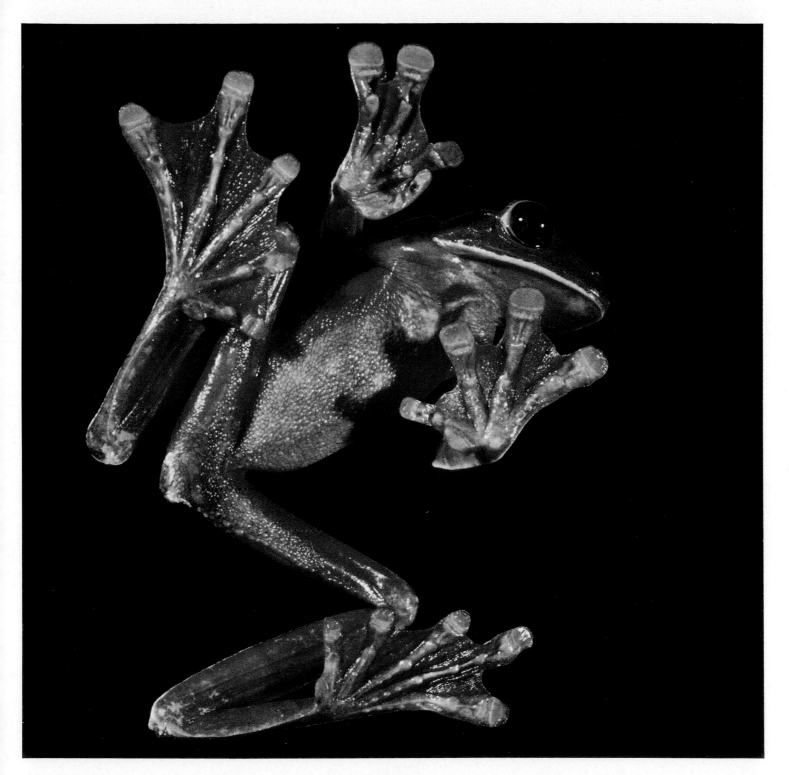

Perfect specimens It is not worth spending time and film taking pictures of flowers or fruits damaged by insects or frost. Always try to find perfect specimens which will be a joy to the beholder. Once a perfect flower is found, never delay taking it, for rain, frost or hailstones can ruin a beautiful bloom within minutes and you'll never get a second chance.

Backlighting enriches colours Red or yellow flowers or leaves look even more dramatic if they are lit from behind so that the colours appear to glow and stand out from their background. Look for red poppies in summer and deciduous leaves in autumn to photogaph in this way.

Use a reflector Close-ups of flowers or fruits can sometimes be improved – especially if taken at a time of day when there are long shadows – by using a reflector to fill-in the shadows. Aluminium cooking foil wrapped around a piece of card makes an inexpensive reflector. Alternatively, there are neat circular reflectors available in white, silver or gold finish which collapse into a small pouch.

People convey scale If people are included in a picture they can give a clear indication of the size of a tree or an architectural feature. When used in this way, people do not need to dominate the picture. Do make sure the colour of their clothing does not clash with any natural colours in the picture.

Taking sequences One of the easiest short-term photo sequences to take is of a large flower opening. An evening primrose flower will open in seconds, but most other flowers take several hours if not days to open. Sequences spanning an even longer time interval include before-and-after pictures of a new garden and also the same scene in different seasons. Remember to note the viewpoint and lens, and refer to the previous picture when taking the next one.

Garden view Wander around your garden with your camera, preferably on a fine day when the light is good. Don't take any pictures at first, but occasionally look through the camera viewfinder, assessing each part of the garden for possible pictures. Spring or summer, when flowers and shrubs are likely to look their best, may be the most suitable time for pictures. But don't rule out other times of year, especially if you have trees and shrubs with good autumn colour, or if you grow winter-flowering shrubs, or want to record seasonal changes in your garden.

Small areas Photographing a small garden may seem easy, but it can be a challenge to find the best viewpoint. Fit a wide-angle lens and shoot from a low viewpoint, perhaps with some colourful flowers in the foreground, to 'increase' the size of the garden visually. Or try a high vantage point, such as a bedroom window.

Close-up Don't concentrate only on capturing a wide expanse of garden. Move in close and record small groups of flowers or plants. Even with simple cameras you can usually shoot as close as 1 metre (3ft) from the subject. The standard lens on an SLR can be focused even closer and you can add special close-up equipment (see 'Close-up lens' on page 72).

Houseplants Many houseplants make attractive subjects. Don't always photograph them where they are in the room. To shoot a small collection of plants, arrange them carefully on a table near a window, shooting from a side angle for best results.

Get to know your area Wander around with your camera and see what sort of flowers and plants you come across in your neighbourhood. Aim to spend a whole day in a particular location – anything from 100 metres (35ft) stretch of hedgerow to a tract of marsh or moorland – and see what varieties you find.

◀ Double herbaceous borders at Crathes Castle, Scotland, taken in early morning light using a 150mm lens on a Hasselblad on Professional Ektachrome 64.

Adding flash You can add a bit of extra sparkle to flower shots by adding flash. Only a small amount of flash is required if you don't want to eliminate the effect of any natural daylight in the picture. First take a meter reading of the subject – this might be 1/125sec at f/11. If you have an automatic flash set it to two stops more than the meter reading – that is, f/5.6 – for a balanced daylight/flash exposure.

Shooting at night If you have to take pictures of plants or flowers at night, flash is the best light source. First shine a torch on the plant so that you can focus accurately; then set the flash to the appropriate setting for a correct exposure. Shooting at night has the advantage that you can eliminate any unattractive background details which would normally be visible in daylight.

In the studio When photographing flowers in a studio, choose a time when they are open and look their best. Arrange them in a vase and choose a plain-coloured background so that they stand out clearly. Try different lighting angles to reveal the shape and texture of the flowers. Flash is the best light source: lamps become very hot and may cause the flowers to wilt. Keep a fine-mist water sprayer handy for freshening the flowers.

In the greenhouse A greenhouse can be a natural outdoor studio. Set up the subject in the best lit part of the greenhouse, using daylight coming through the panes. You can shoot in direct sunlight, but you may need to soften the light by covering the glass with special diffusing material. Use white reflectors to fill-in any shadow details.

Flower-heads If you own an SLR camera you won't have to buy special close-up equipment for more detailed shots. The standard 50mm lens on a 35mm SLR can usually focus down to about 0.45m (1ft), which is close enough to photograph a small bunch of flowers, or a large flower-head.

Real macro If you intend to do a lot of close-ups of flowers and plants, consider buying a macro lens instead of a normal standard lens. A macro lens gives a magnification of half life-size reproduction (life size is × 1). This is close enough for recording small flower heads, leaves in close-up, and so on. As well as a standard 55mm macro you can buy longer 105 and 200mm versions for close-up work taken from a distance of insects on flowers.

Zoom macro If you can get hold of a zoom lens with a 'macro' facility you can focus more closely than with a conventional zoom (although not as close as with a real macro lens), and you will be able to photograph most of the parts of the flowers and plants in reasonable detail.

Add a close-up lens Convert your standard lens for close-ups by adding a supplementary close-up lens. This looks like a filter and simply screws onto the front of the lens. Such supplementary lenses are available in different magnification strengths, depending on how close you want to photograph. Buy a variable close-up lens for a range of magnification strengths in one easy-to-use optic.

Extended close-up To avoid diminishing optical clarity, which is inevitable when you use a supplementary close up lens. Try a set of extension tubes or a bellows extension. Both these accessories fit between the camera body and the lens and allow a variable degree of magnification. A bellows extension can be adjusted to any magnification point within its range and is less restricting to use than tubes. Both types provide extremely close-up detail, but camera and subject must be kept perfectly still during focusing and exposure: even the slightest movement will result in a blurred picture. Always use a tripod for detailed close-ups.

Rigid support All macro photography calls for a firmly supported camera – slight movement can ruin a close-up shot. You can use a good tripod or, when shooting indoors, try a small table-top tripod. This is ideal for photographing house plants or flowers on top of a table. Make sure you lock the adjustment controls on the tripod before each shot, otherwise the camera may slip out of focus.

Local parks Try visiting your local park for shots of flowers and plants. Most parks are well stocked with interesting varieties, and when they are in bloom you can record a wide expanse of colour, often with an ornamental pond, trees and greensward.

Botanical gardens This type of garden offers one special advantage to the photographer – greenhouses full of rare and exotic plants. Look for strong shape or colour in the plants you photograph – ferns, palms and cacti all make interesting subjects. Try to choose a bright but slightly cloudy day for best light – you may find the greenhouse glass overhead acts as a useful natural diffuser for the light. If you come in from the cold, wait until your camera lens de-mists before taking pictures.

Woods and forests Gardens are not the only places offering good plant life – there is plenty to be found in wood and forest areas. Look for interesting plants in and around trees. Light can be a problem in heavily wooded areas, particularly when the trees are in leaf. Shoot in autumn when the foliage is less dense and the colours are more varied.

Ponds, lakes and rivers Look for interesting flower and plant life wherever there is water. Most ponds are quite still and you can record lilies and other surface plants quite easily. Use a polarising filter over the lens to minimise reflections. Seek out plants on the edge of a river or lake

and use the passing water or wavelets as an effective background. Set the camera on a tripod and use a slow shutter speed (about 1/8sec) to record the movement of the river water as a blurred flow.

Underwater plants You don't have to be a sub-aqua diver to record underwater plants: you can shoot through the surface of the water. Place the camera face down into a glass bottomed box or small plastic fish tank. Pre-set the focusing to the approximate distance away from the plants and set for an automatic exposure. Make sure you work in clear water and avoid air bubbles on the camera container.

Urban plant life You will find many plants and flowers in built-up areas. You might come across an unexpected display of flowers in someone's window-box or in a courtyard garden among tall concrete buildings. Even where plants have been covered by concrete paving, you may find some appearing between cracks – plant power is amazingly strong. Ruined buildings are invariably host to an abundance of wild flowers – sometimes including quite rare species.

▲ Spines on the flowering spikes of a spaniard *Aciphylla scott-thomsonii* are highlighted by back lighting late in the day on the lower slopes of Mt. Cook in New Zealand. A Hasselblad with a 150mm lens was used on Professional Ektachrome 64.

Finding suitable subjects Look through any book on flowers or plants and you will see there is an abundant choice of subject matter. Look in your own garden first – if you don't have the kind of species you would like to photograph, consider planting them for next year. Try some of the different locations mentioned earlier, photograph as many varieties as possible and see which ones make the most pleasing subjects to photograph.

Specific plants Set a theme for your plant photograph by recording the most attractive garden varieties of a particular species, such as a rose. Gardening books will help you to identify and locate various species, and you can make a long-term project of building up a collection of your plant photographs.

Access problems Some plants and flowers, particularly wild varieties, can be difficult to photograph because of their remote location. Be prepared to do a lot of walking or climbing to get access to less well known plants. You may wish to restrict the equipment you carry to a minimum if you have a long trek to reach your subject.

Perfect bloom Find out when flowers are likely to be in perfect bloom for pictures. In the open, this is likely to be a certain short period in either spring or summer. Note down some possible dates, but remember that weather conditions can make a difference. With cut flowers, shoot after a day or so when they have had a chance to open up properly.

Mass of flowers When shooting a group of flowers, try a few different approaches. Fit a wide-angle lens to take in a wide area of flower bed – this will emphasise the shape and colour design. Or move in close to a single stem and let neighbouring flowers act as a colourful backdrop. With any group, try and focus on a central point.

◀ Autumnal leaves of a maple – *Acer japonicum* 'Vitifolium' – trans-illuminated by the sun, were taken with a Hasselblad, using a 150mm lens and Professional Ektachrome.

Time-lapse You can record a flower opening and closing over a period of time by using a time-lapse technique. Place the flower in front of a plain background and set a camera and flashgun on a tripod (the flash can be set at an angle to the camera if required). Then simply take a shot at regular intervals say, every hour or two, either manually or by using a timing device. The result will be a series of pictures of the bloom opening and closing.

Trees It is easy to ignore trees when searching for subjects to photograph, but they can be very interesting. There are plenty of varieties to be found in parkland, open countryside, woodland, forest areas and special aboreta. Choose your viewpoint carefully and try picking out individual trees for pictures. Autumn is often the best time because the colours are more varied. A long lens helps to isolate tree detail from the background. Also, try looking upwards with a wide-angle to record a span of branches against a bright blue sky.

Leaves Move in close to photograph the leaves on a tree. Overhanging branches are easiest to shoot, otherwise some climbing will be necessary. Backlighting will reveal the shape, colour and texture of the leaves best. Look for different coloured leaves in autumn, not just on the branches, but on the ground after they have fallen.

Fungi There is a wide variety of fungi to be found in damp wooded areas. You will find them growing on and around trees – sulphur fungus around beech, for example. In these shaded areas the available daylight is often low so be prepared to use a tripod. Angled lighting helps reveal the shape and detail of the fungus.

Fruits and seeds Don't discard flowers after they have wilted – their seeds and fruits can make pleasing pictures. Photograph them on the flowers or when they have fallen to the ground. Look for fallen fruits in wooded areas – horse-chestnuts on a large bed of colourful autumn leaves, for instance.

Plants and insects Insects on plants and flowers add extra interest and scale to the picture. Close-up equipment will be needed for most tiny insects, although you should be able to record, say, a butterfly on a flower-head with a standard lens. Move in carefully so as not to frighten the insect away.

Keep a record Take a notebook with you when photographing plants and flowers and record what you have taken. When you take a lot of pictures of different species over a short period of time the notes will help you identify them after processing. Write down the film frame numbers (say, 1 to 36) and record the relevant botanical details (if known) next to each frame taken.

Good labelling Using your notes, lay out your pictures in the sequence taken and mark on them the names of each flower and plant. Keen horticulturists will want to use the botanical names. Use small sticky labels for both slides and prints: do not write on the print itself or the writing may show through or become smudged if the paper is the conventional resin-coated type.

Blow ups If you examine your picture and find that the camera was not close enough to the main subject, remember it is possible to enlarge a certain section of the picture area at the printing stage. This can be done from either a slide or a negative. If it is a print, mark out the area you want enlarged and take the print and negative to the processor and ask for a sectional enlargement. With a slide, where there is no original print, draw a rough diagram showing the area of enlargement. There may be some loss of image quality, depending on how sharp and well-exposed the enlarged area is.

ADAM WOOLFITT

Adam Woolfitt began his professional career in a studio specializing in promotional photography for record sleeves. Today his assignments for major British and American book and magazine publishers take him all over the world. The photographs of buildings in the following pages demonstrate his mastery of composition and his creative use of light.

Allow enough time   You won't get good pictures if you are running around trying to keep pace with a tour group or friends on a visit to some beautiful town or castle. Go alone or with another photographer who won't rush you.

Study your subject carefully   Many buildings are not so wonderfully sited and finding a really good viewpoint is difficult and time-consuming. Both cities and landscapes can be cluttered up with electric wires, lamp-posts, and so on – which could ruin your shots.

Carry the right equipment   On 35mm an 80-200mm zoom lens is excellent for details or longer shots of buildings within their landscape. A wide-angle lens (28mm or, better still, 24mm) is essential if you want to tackle architecture seriously.

Use your wide-angle with caution!   If you point the camera upwards, parallel lines will converge; if you hold the camera level, you may have too much foreground. The solution to the problem is either to fill the foreground of the picture with things like flower-beds or water such as a pool or lake; or to invest (heavily) in a shift lens, which lets you frame the buildings without tilting the camera.

Learn about light   If you want really good results you must learn to wait for suitable light and weather. Indeed, you may have to visit the location several times at different hours of the day and even in different seasons of the year before it all 'comes right'.

Choose an appropriate film   Slower films (ISO 100) will generally give sharper results with less grain. When shooting slides indoors you may need an artificial-light film if most of the illumination comes from electric lights. Only use high-speed films (ISO 1200) when you have insufficient light to prevent camera or subject movement at your chosen f/stop.

Beware reflections!   Flash pointed *straight* at flat shiny surfaces will bounce *straight* back, spoiling the pictures with flare or reflections. When shooting glass showcases or oil paintings, work from an angle; or, if you must shoot from directly in front, use a flash extension lead and place your light to one side of the reflecting surface.

Watch the contrast!   Large rooms are much brighter near the windows. The most even light occurs at mid-day, when the summer sun is directly overhead and bounces light up onto the ceiling. Compose carefully, to exclude strongly lighted areas of floor, or windows showing the sky: these areas will be many times brighter than the rest of the scene and the film won't be able to handle so much contrast.

Hold the camera level   You can obtain two-way spirit levels which fit into the accessory shoe for really accurate work. I prefer to use focusing screens with a fine etched cross-grid to help me align the building verticals.

Always carry a folding mini-tripod   If you get caught out, improvise! A pile of prayer books can level a camera in a cathedral; or a few coins will hold the lens level on a mantlepiece. I once slung my Nikon between two ski poles for a one-second exposure.

Paint a room   If you like a challenge, try painting a large room with flashes. Shoot at night with a tripod and compose with the lights on. Use a flashgun with an 'open' flash facility and a quick re-cycle time. Turn off the lights, open the shutter on 'time' and then walk around lighting each area with individual flashes. Experiment with 5-8 flashes on ISO 100 film at f/5.6 before closing the shutter. With some luck and a bit of practice you can light a very large area using only a small flashgun in this way.

◀ Bull Wharf on the Thames shot for the LWT calendar in late evening light (November), using a Nikon F2 with 180mm f/2.8 lens at 1/15 f/4 (hand held) on Kodachrome 64.

▲ The water gate of a Venetian palace, shot for the *Sunday Telegraph Magazine* using a Nikon F3 with 105mm f/4 lens at 1/60 f/4 on Kodachrome 64.

Exterior composition Every subject contains elements of good composition – the trick is to make them work photographically. These elements include line, shape, texture, volume, light and shade. Choose the ideal viewpoint and use shadows to emphasise line, depth, and mass in your composition, following the path of the sun. Think about the relationship between your subject and the surrounding space. Start with simple shapes, making them the centre of interest.

Viewpoint Determine your viewpoint by walking around the building to discover its interesting faces and surface details. Next, decide on distance based on foreground and background interest and choice of lens. Experiment by tilting the camera. If using a wide-angle lens, beware the distortion that occurs when the camera tilts off the horizontal. If you can't avoid tilting, do it emphatically, so that lines converge steeply – gentle convergence just looks wrong.

Urban buildings The disadvantage of cities is that they're busy, and offer less space and opportunity to frame buildings carefully. But you can get up high quite easily. Get to know a city on foot, noting the variety and contrast in architectural styles, and pay attention to how light and shadow make buildings and features prominent at different times of day.

Architecture in landscape Look for harmony and conflict between man-made structures and the natural world in the countryside. Hills and vistas of sky offer sweeping backgrounds, while animals, flowers and pathways provide varied foreground interest. Use a wide-angle lens to take advantage of every detail – but watch for intruding power lines or aircraft.

Timing On location many things can ruin picture-making. Increase your chances of success by timing your location shots. Get to know when a factory chimney expels smoke. Check local newspapers for events concerning buildings. For example, certain villages stage traditional 'ringing' ceremonies in which children join hands to encircle the church. Find out about the plans for and progress of restoration or demolition of major buildings and be ready to record any changes.

Picture ideas Once you've decided on a building to photograph, ask yourself if the subject suggests special treatment. Try the traditional approach to shooting a stately home or a ruined abbey, perhaps as a painter might have depicted them. For instance, pictures of buildings in the classical or Georgian style should emphasise the lines of perspective. Certain landmarks won't look impressive without their environs. Alternatively, single features can reveal much about a building – like the rose window or fan vaulting in a cathedral. Be aware of conventions – but at the same time try to avoid clichés.

Direction of light Anticipating the angle of light saves time on location and offers compositional options. Find out which way a building faces, then draw a diagram with it relative to the four points of the compass. Trace the path of the sun, remembering the season: in midsummer it is at its highest, making very short shadows at mid-day; at about the turn of the year it is at its lowest, reaching scarcely half-way up the southern sky at noon. In the afternoon an east-facing façade will darken as the sun descends behind it, while façades facing west will be in shadow until later in the afternoon. Take extra care to avoid backlighting and low sunlight that casts your own shadow into view.

All weather A serious architectural photographer will use the special advantages of seasonal weather. Dead leaves in a churchyard, snow melting on a cottage roof, lightning over a ruined building – conditions such as these imbue subjects with a special atmosphere. Capture an invisible breeze by means of the foliage of trees that surround a solid building: load the camera with film rated with the lowest ISO number, set it on a tripod, and keep the shutter open for several seconds, using a small aperture. In snow always select at least one stop more than the meter suggests. Under clear, cloudless skies snow may reflect an excessively blue cast onto subjects in the photograph – but this can be corrected by filtration. (See Filters, page 105.)

At night Tall floodlit or interior-lit buildings make fascinating colour subjects. Pictures of buildings that are illuminated from below may appear too dark at the top, even when correctly exposed. Use a colour-correction filter to render fluorescent light correctly on colour film. Care is necessary with the unpredictable effects of long-duration exposures for night photography; a tripod and a steady surface are essential. Expose colour film for up to twice as long as the meter recommends and bracket your exposures. If your camera has a multiple-exposure facility try balancing interior lighting and any available twilight. Without moving the camera, make the initial exposure of the building and sky, calculated for at least three stops less than metered. Include the lights of moving traffic in the foreground to create a 'streaking' effect, red tail lights will make dramatic streaks as cars drive away.

Changing tone Alter the balance of light and shade in b & w by using coloured filters. The rule is that any filter lightens the tone of a colour similar to it, while simultaneously darkening the opposite colour. Thus, a yellow filter darkens blue skies, but it lightens the colour of foliage; a blue filter darkens red brick, but lightens a cloudless sky.

Useful colour filters The most useful compensating filters for architectural work on colour film are the polariser and the 81A. A polariser darkens blue skies and eliminates reflections. The 81A 'warms' a blue cast or cool-looking subjects. Fit a graduated filter, available in various colours, to tint skies. For hazy effects use a soft-focus filter. The TTL meter in your SLR automatically compensates for filter exposure.

Film tolerance Colour and black-and-white negative films are more tolerant to exposure errors than transparency films. Experiment with colour infrared film to produce bizarre results.

Sharpness Fit the camera on to a solid tripod – preferably one with a built-in spirit level – and use a cable release to fire the shutter. If possible, use a small aperture for maximum depth of field. Avoid photographing in heavy wind or traffic which could vibrate the camera during exposure times of 1/60sec and less. Telephoto lenses are most sensitive to shake. If you hand-hold the camera, support your body on a firm upright and hold your breath during exposure.

Buildings in focus Pictures of buildings demand sharpness from the foreground to the background, so wide-angle lenses are generally ideal. Within limits, a standard 35mm lens causes relatively little perspective distortion if it is tilted off a strictly horizontal position. Remember that the problem of sharp focus can be considerably eased if you use the smallest aperture possible, since it will provide the maximum depth of field.

Scale To judge architectural scale, just count the number of storeys in a building or compare the height of a steeple to the height of the walls. To show the scale of a building, try to include people or a familiar object such as a car. A photograph of a stately home implies that it is set in large grounds; but if a lesser dwelling has exotic surroundings they should be shown to indicate whether the house dominates the environment or is hidden.

Camera shift If you try to fit more of a building into frame by tilting the camera upwards, the verticals converge. Straighten verticals by elevating the camera position or by using an expensive shift (or perspective-correction) lens. These are made in 28mm and 35mm focal lengths and imitate the rising front effect of a large view camera. The lens moves upwards in its mount, but the film stays perpendicular to the building. Used horizontally the shift can correct a dramatically receding wall or remove an obstruction without the need to change viewpoint. Downward shift can be used with aerial viewpoints.

Panoramas Try a panoramic view to show a building in its environment. Set up a camera on a level tripod with a panhead, then decide where your panorama begins and ends. Pan the camera, take a sequence of views, letting each overlap slightly into the preceding picture. For continuity try to keep the sky and lighting even. Align the final prints in sequence, trim off the excess overlaps, and mount on stiff card.

Dominating foregrounds Ideally, foreground details direct the eye towards the main subject in a picture; but sometimes foreground object dominate. Look for lines and patterns that draw attention to a building in mid-distance – paths, shadows and cobblestones, for example. Lenses of 28mm and wider make foreground objects loom relatively large, and some overlooked details can become unwelcome features in the finished print. On the other hand, you can use a macro or telephoto lens to focus on a foreground subject, such as a dew-spangled spider's web, with a modern building providing the background.

Negative space In most architectural photographs background is negative space, surrounding the dominant shape of the subject. Telephoto lenses can create new relationships between objects miles apart by the effect of compressing perspective. A cemetery in the foreground can be made to dominate a power station in the distance, for example. *Never* let the background distract attention from the subject.

Rule of thirds The sky may occupy up to two thirds of an architectural photograph, so use its compositional possibilities to advantage; think of the superb cloudscapes in the paintings of Constable. The worst effects of dully overcast skies can be tempered by a warm graduated filter. A range of filters for black-and-white films can be used to darken skies.

Line and rhythm Straight lines dominate the world of architecture. Lines are crucial in composing an architectural photograph. They lead the eye to the centre of interest and they have symbolic meanings – the vertical lines in a church draw the eye heavenwards. Be sensitive to the rhythmic interplay of lines and surfaces and tones. Notice how the hard, severely functional lines of a modern building contrast with the more intricate lines and softly weathered stonework of old churches and other old buildings.

An eye for detail Architectural features such as brickwork, archways, gargoyles, inscriptions, and so on make fascinating pictures. The best light is angled sunlight because it throws textures into relief and exaggerates form. With colour film, use a polarising filter that deepens tonality and coarsens textures in the photograph. In overcast conditions, and when shooting indoors, use an angled flashgun set at full power, but use a wide aperture to allow any available daylight to register in the picture.

Comparison and contrast In older cities different styles and types of architecture are lumped haphazardly together. You can point up this random collection of contrasting shapes by using a powerful telephoto lens; or you can create a sense of order from this chaos by, for instance, isolating a statue against the façade of a modern office block or other building. See how you can compare and contrast old and new found in the environment.

Macro architecture Use macro photography in architecture to photograph small models, or to record fine detail – inscriptions on brass plaques and wood carvings, for instance. With macro lenses and attachments you are hampered by a very shallow depth of field, so work methodically and take special care with focusing to ensure the best results.

▶ Detail of a library in Finland designed by Alvar Aalto. Shot in the early morning using a Nikon F2 on a tripod with 28mm shift lens and polarising filter at 1/15 f/11 on Kodachrome 64.

▲ St Paul's Cathedral, the College of Arms and the 'Welsh' Church, shot for the German magazine *Geo*, using a Nikon F3 with 15mm f/3.5 lens at 1/30 f/11 on Kodachrome 64.

Architecture and fantasy Use architecture as one part of a double exposure, or a slide sandwich. To create an illusion of a lighted-up building against a fantasy sky first take a photograph of a starlit sky, or a randomly perforated black card back lit. Then reload, ensuring that the film isn't out of register, find a building surrounded by even black space (or shoot at night), and expose the roll again, bracketing exposures throughout. To make slide sandwiches put two thinly exposed transparencies together in the same slide mount and project for effect.

Creative reflection Use reflective surfaces to emphasise symmetry in architecture, or to introduce objects into the composition that lie outside the frame. Some modern architecture with mirrored façades reflects surrounding skies and buildings. Be careful that the amount of light from the reflected image isn't greater or less than that of the background. Water makes an interesting foreground to architecture. An exposure time of several seconds records motion on the water and reproduces an exotic reflection of the sharply defined building.

Useful shadow   Shadows can be used to hide unwanted details. If a background is so obtrusive that it threatens to overwhelm the picture subject, observe it at different times to see if shadows will obscure it or soften its effect. If there's a broken window pane in a house you want to photograph, wait for side lighting to put it in shadow. Visit a location at various times of day and in different light.

Interior design   Interiors of buildings can contain interesting architectural details, such as staircases, vaulting, wood-carving, stained glass, and objects of furniture. All such things can be used to convey atmosphere or set a mood.

Available interior light   With black-and-white film you can mix daylight and electric lamplight. Balancing these is more difficult with colour film; try to match your daylight or tungsten type film with the predominant light source, and ensure that colour casts from unbalanced light sources don't affect the film colour. Fit a colour-correction filter to convert tungsten film for use in daylight, and vice versa. Soften direct window light with a shade or curtains. The best-lit façade usually faces north, lit from a south-facing window.

Additional interior lighting   Small interiors lit by conventional light bulbs are often very dim, requiring exposures too long to hand-hold the camera. The obvious solution is to use a tripod, but sometimes this is inconvenient. One way to get round the problem is to replace the bulbs with photoflood lamps, which give out several times more light. Take care, though, when using photofloods in ordinary sockets, because they get very hot: switch the lamps on just long enough to make the exposure.

Interior composition   Locate a point of interest around which to compose. Draw the viewer's eye in by keeping well-lit areas near the centre of the picture, and allow shadows to deepen towards the edge of the frame. If strong contrasts arise expose for lighter shadows, then bracket. Err on the side of over-exposure. Always watch out for your own image in mirrors, glossy walls, windows, glazed doors, and other reflective surfaces. Keep the foreground in proportion, elevating the camera to reduce the foreground if necessary.

Stained glass   To photograph stained-glass windows, bright overcast daylight behind the window is ideal. Take your meter reading from a piece of glass of average tone and density for an overall exposure. Be careful not to aim the camera upwards to create converging verticals. A very large window may be recorded in sections then reconstructed.

▼ Reflection of Amsterdam houses in a canal, shot for *National Geographic Magazine*, using a Nikon F3 with 35mm f/1.4 lens at 1/60 f/8 on Kodachrome 64.

STEPHEN DALTON

Stephen Dalton, one of the leading British exponents of insect and bird photography, has spent many years perfecting his skills and, in particular, developing special equipment for photographing fast-moving subjects. He has won numerous awards for his work, which has appeared in many magazines and books, notably his own *Caught in Motion* and *Secret Lives*.

► Mediterranean chameleon catching a fly, shot using a Hasselblad with 135mm lens at 1/25,000 f/16, on Professional Kodachrome 120.

Welfare of subject   The most important thing to remember when photographing wildlife is to place the welfare of the animal before the photograph. Avoid subjecting any creature to more stress than is absolutely necessary. Birds are particularly prone, if frightened, to desert their nests and young, so nest photography should never be attempted by anyone who is not familiar with the techniques involved or the idiosyncracies of the species. Flash photography may frighten some animals.

Know your subject   Whenever possible become familiar with the animal you are working with by reading about and observing its habits before using your camera. Understanding and anticipating the behaviour of the animal – so that you know what to expect – is one of the secrets to successful wildlife photography, and is much more useful than an encyclopaedic knowledge of photographic techniques.

Interest   Pictures of animals *doing* something are more interesting than straight portraits. Try to show action of some sort – running, flying, jumping, feeding, fighting, courtship or play. Equally worth capturing on film are the less active aspects of nature such as camouflage, warning coloration, or some behavioural trait. If you have to make do with a portrait photograph, make sure it's a good one by clever use of lighting and composition.

Near or far   Getting close to your subject with a medium focal-length lens, perhaps by using a hide or stalking, generally produces technically better results than by employing massive telephoto lenses. Watching animals from close quarters is certainly more exciting than viewing from afar. If you are able to get very close to your subject without distressing it, a wide-angle shot may be most effective to capture both the animal and its natural habitat.

Composition Become aware of lines and shapes in the picture area, making them work for you to improve picture design. Avoid cluttered and confusing backgrounds; sometimes these are difficult to get away from in nature. Whenever possible move around your subject until you find the best viewpoint. The key to good composition in animal photography is simplicity.

Natural lighting Study the effects of lighting and notice how it can totally change the mood of a scene. Back or side lighting is nearly always far more attractive than flat lighting when the sun is behind the camera. Early morning is a wonderful time for nature photography. Texture is enhanced by the oblique direction of light, sunlit objects have a warm glow, and often the shadows are touched with blue. Fog, mist and dew add exciting possibilities for early morning shots. It is also the best time to see a wide variety of animals.

Flash pitfalls Electronic flash is a very convenient way of providing portable light, and within limits it arrests both subject movements and camera shake. However, unless used with discretion flash can produce ghastly results. The main aim should be to try to make the animal look as though it is lit with natural light. Avoid the flat lifeless effect of having the main light anywhere near the lens axis – keep it well to one side and use fill-in whenever necessary. Also, unless the animal is nocturnal, avoid jet-black backgrounds (remember that light intensity falls off with the square of the distance).

In the studio There are times when animals are best photographed indoors rather than in the wild. Some insects and cold-blooded creatures, for example, are more easily handled in the studio, and are perfectly happy in captivity. In such cases, though, a thorough knowledge of the subject is vital, for not only does its

natural habitat have to be reconstructed on the table-top, but the captive has to look at home within it. Do not forget to release the creature exactly where you found it as soon as possible.

Close-up Modern macro lenses make it easy to focus close-up to insects and other small creatures. As with telephoto lenses, the extra magnification increases the risks of camera shake, particularly at small apertures, so it is sensible to use some form of camera support. Flash eliminates this problem but requires sensitive handling – remember to avoid black backgrounds, flat lighting and large areas of shadows.

High-speed photography So called 'computer' flash guns can be used to reduce or arrest the image movement of rapidly moving animals such as flying insects and birds. Choose a flash unit which can be manually switched down to low power – the lower the power the higher the speed. By selecting 1/8 or 1/16 power, a speed of 1/5,000-1/10,000sec may be obtained, but bear in mind that the light output is reduced proportionately. Thus it will be necessary to enlarge the lens aperture by several stops or to use a faster film than normally.

Capturing the right moment As it is difficult or often impossible to gauge the exact moment for firing the camera, an optical trigger is best employed, so that the animal itself fires the camera shutter when it breaks the light beam. There are a number of such units on the market. Remember that camera shutters take between 1/10-1/20 second to open and that this long delay has to be taken into account when setting up the beam and photo-cell, otherwise the creature may be completely out of focus or out of the picture. The delay can be eliminated by using open flash, but this technique can be used only when the ambient light level is very subdued.

Birds Look out for birds visiting your garden, particularly during the winter months when there is less food about. Set up a cat-proof bird table with scraps of food and nut dispensers hanging on it for the birds to peck at. You can then photograph them at eye level from a discreet distance, using a telephoto or zoom lens in the 80-200mm range to catch close up detail. Shoot from behind a house window or through a small hole cut in a nearby shed.

Birds in flight Photographing birds in mid-air requires fast reflexes. First, take a light reading from the sky and pre-set the exposure for one stop more than indicated (to capture detail.) Pre-focus the lens (usually at infinity) and use as fast a shutter speed as possible (at least 1/500sec) to 'freeze' the motion of the wings.

Small insects Find small insects to photograph on garden flowers and plants, as well as under top layers of soil.

▲ A blue-tit photographed using a Leicaflex with 100mm macro Elinan lens at 1/25,000 f/11 on Kodachrome 25.

Zoo photography You can photograph a wide variety of animals on a one-day visit to the zoo. Most zoos permit photographers to take pictures of the animals. Choose a day when the zoo may not have many visitors, perhaps in mid-week, so you can wander around without being jostled.

Restrictions Look out for notices which restrict the use of photography – they are important for your safety as well as for the well-being of the zoo residents. Don't use flash where this is forbidden – you may frighten the animals. And don't set up a tripod where it is likely to obstruct the public walkways.

Open spaces Some of the larger zoo animals – bears, lions, tigers, etc. – are allowed to roam around in large open pits so that visitors can look down at them without bars to obstruct the view. You'll need a long focal length (200mm or more) to get in close enough to record the animals' heads. When they are moving around, a zoom will allow you to frame the pictures more exactly.

In cages When photographing caged animals, you can practically eliminate the bars by making sure the subject is a reasonable distance away from them. Use a telephoto lens, focus normally, and select a wide aperture (around f/5.6 or wider) so that, with the lens focused on the subject, the depth of field will be limited enough to throw the cage bars out of focus.

Safari parks In most safari parks you are restricted to viewing, and photographing, the animals from the safety of your car. *Never open the windows to take pictures if this is prohibited.* Use a long lens and press it up against the window glass to minimise reflection; it helps if you have cleaned the car windows before setting out.

◀ A lion club photographed in Kenya, using a Nikon FE2.

In the countryside If you want camouflage but don't want to go to the trouble of building your own hide, try using a net covered in leaves, branches and other natural materials. Lie down and drape the net over you, leaving space to point the camera through. Or hide behind a tree tying one side of the net to the trunk and draping the rest over your head. A small folding seat aids comfort. Put black tape over any shiny metallic parts of your cameras and lenses.

Permanent hide If you are really enthusiastic you may wish to construct your own permanent hide. You can buy metal-framed hides with spy-holes for photography, or you can build your own from natural materials (wooden stakes, covered in netting and branches).

Mobile hide Use your car as a mobile hide. Park near to woodland or other wildlife areas and shoot through an open window, resting the camera on the window frame. Use a special window clamp to support the camera if needed. A tent draped with camouflage can easily be moved into position and allows extra room and comfort for the photographer.

Through glass When you take pictures of subjects behind glass, make sure the glass is clean. Watch out for reflections, particularly from angled glass which can pick up details of any overhead lights. Use a polarising filter over the lens to reduce reflection. If flash is permitted, shoot from an angle (not straight on) or hold the flashgun off-camera to avoid the light reflecting back into the camera lens.

Difficult lighting Inside animal houses you may come across a variety of lighting problems. If the light level is low, you may need flash. If this isn't permitted, a fast film (ISO 400 or faster) will be needed; you may not be able to use a tripod for long exposures with slower film. If fluorescent lighting is in use it may produce a green colour cast on ordinary daylight-balanced colour film. However with colour negatives, the unwanted tint can be removed at the printing stage.

Activity time Keep a look out for the most interesting pictures at feeding times. Monkeys and seals, in particular, have a lot of fun when feeding and you may get shots of the keepers involved with the activity, too. Elephants being bathed can also yield some good shots, from the subjects as well as from the crowd.

Planning a field trip Choose your location carefully. Study large-scale Ordnance Survey maps and, if necessary, visit the spot without your camera to familiarise yourself with the terrain. Make a list of what equipment is needed, particularly lenses. Read about the subjects you intend to photograph – knowledge of their behaviour at various times of the year will help you time your trip for best results.

▼ An eland, photographed in Kenya with a Nikon FE2 with a 400mm lens at 1/60 f/5.6.

Legal aspects   Before you go out into the field to take pictures, consider the legal aspects. Is the land open to the public? Is photography permitted? Do any conservation laws forbid photography of certain species? Remember that many of these restrictions were adopted because of cruelty and are designed to protect the wildlife you are trying to photograph. Don't break the law just for the sake of a few pictures.

Field accessories   Keep accessories to a minimum on a field trip, especially if you are likely to have to do a lot of walking or climbing to the location. Too much heavy equipment will be a hindrance rather than a help. Restrict lenses to two or three – a wide-angle, a medium range zoom, and a long telephoto are sufficient to cover most wildlife. A few filters can be helpful, such as a polariser or skylight, but special-effect filters are considered 'not on'. A tripod and cable release are essential in wildlife photography. For photographing birds and other shy animals, binoculars are a must.

Stalking animals   To avoid setting up a special hide, try stalking animals. Before your trip study the habits of the animals you wish to photograph and when you are likely to capture the most interesting activity; dawn and sunset are often best times. Good stalkers should know where to find the animals in the first place. Approach animals cautiously and be ready to shoot them if they suddenly set off on the move.

Long wait   Even with the best preparation you can spend many unproductive hours waiting to catch a good shot of your photographic 'prey'. Wildlife can be unpredictable, so you need a lot of patience and determination. Be sure to take a supply of food and drink to help you pass the hours. Don't forget a bag so you can keep all your rubbish together. Also, don't forget to take it away.

Arrive early   If the 'early bird catches the worm', the early photographer certainly has more chance of catching the best pictures. If you arrive in the field early and set up before your subject is likely to appear, there is a better chance of your not being noticed. Once settled, stay where you are and wait for the subject(s) to turn up on the scene.

Baiting   Animals and birds are attracted by food. If you can lay down some food as bait at a reasonable distance from the camera, there is likely to be some activity to photograph before long. Learn as much as you can about animal and bird feeding habits, and choose the bait most likely to attract those you are planning to photograph.

◄ A badger crossing a stream, photographed using a Hasselblad with a 150mm Zeiss Sonnar lens at 1/1000 on Ektachrome.

Remote control This allows you to take pictures when you are some distance from the camera. Place a camera fitted with an autowinder or motordrive on to a tripod and connect a long cable-release to the shutter button. Press the button on the other end of the release each time you want to take a shot; then the film will be automatically advanced, quickly ready for the next exposure.

Infrared beam You can also fire the camera from a distance by using an infrared remote-control unit. Fit the receiver to the camera's shutter release button and hide within firing range of the camera, using the hand-held infrared control unit to trigger it for each shot. Or you can set up an infrared beam emitter and receiver in the path of the camera. When the subject breaks the beam the circuit automatically triggers the camera: the photographer doesn't even have to be at the location.

Flash throw When using flash – for photographing in low light or at night – you may need a flashgun with a good range for distant subjects. Choose a unit with a 'zoom head' which extends the light beam into a longer, narrower beam when using long lens.

Infrared film Use infrared film to photograph wildlife at night. An infrared flashgun emits light which is invisible to the naked eye – but the effects can be seen on infrared film.

Mountains There are plenty of opportunities for capturing wildlife in mountain areas. You can find mountain goats, sheep and other wild animals even in remote areas. Use a long-focal-length lens to isolate the subject, particularly when stalking. A skylight filter should be taken to reduce the effects of haze when taking photographs of animals at a high altitude. Take the minimum of equipment in a back pack with a waterproof cover.

Extreme cold In snow covered regions the extreme cold and harshness of the conditions can offer the wildlife photographer the greatest challenge. Camouflage is difficult in snow, so photograph your subjects behind a small white screen with a hole cut in it for the camera lens. To capture animal detail in snow overexpose by at least a couple of f/stops. Cover metal parts of the camera with tape to prevent them freezing to your skin in extreme cold.

In the heat In the extreme heat in some countries, particularly those with desert areas, wildlife photography presents many problems. Because of the heat you may be able to shoot only in the very early hours of the morning and just before sunset. In any case, most animal activity takes place at these times, and the light will be low enough to reveal interesting textures. Keep all your equipment and film in a 'cool' box or use an aluminium case that will reflect the heat; never use a black case of any type, which will absorb heat.

Rain forests Many of the great tropical rain forest areas support an incredible abundance of bird, reptile and insect life. Light levels tend to be low in dense forest, so look for clearings or river banks. Humidity can be very harmful to your film and equipment so keep them in a case with a good secure seal. Place silica gel inside the case to absorb the excessive moisture.

Sea and seashore Look for interesting sea life near the shore. Seagulls, which look interesting in photographs, are prominent on most shorelines and often fly and settle in groups. Look for marine creatures such as crabs in rock pools.

Underground Visit underground caves for interesting forms of wildlife. Inhabitants can include bats, cave shrimps, salamanders and insects. Caves are dark places so unless you plan to work in the natural light of a cave entrance, always take along a flash.

Aquarium fish Fish in a tank swim rapidly out of the frame and out of focus. You can get round the problem by lowering a sheet of glass into the water to restrict the fish to a shallow area at front of the tank. Then you can set the camera's focusing scale to a fixed distance, and just concentrate on framing.

In flight Use a covered tank to record insects in flight. A glass panel over the top of the tank will allow light from the flash to pass through. An infrared triggering device should be used to capture the subject as it passes in front of the camera: when the subject breaks the beam the exposure will be made automatically. Once the tank is set up the photographer can leave the insect to take the photograph itself.

Photomicrography Insects and other small forms can make fascinating images when photographed under a microscope. You can fit most SLR cameras to a microscope using a simple adaptor. Place the subject on a glass and, using a strong light, focus through the viewfinder. For best colour quality, change the lamp for a flashgun when ready to shoot. Experiment with several exposures to see which gives the best result. If you use tungsten light to illuminate the subject, you'll need to fit a blue 80A filter over the lens or your pictures will have a colour cast.

REFERENCE SECTION

CAMERAS

BUYING A CAMERA

Before you part with any money for a new camera, ask yourself a few pertinent questions. What can I realistically afford? Do I want a simple snapshot camera? Do I want a camera which will stretch my photographic ability? Do I want to be able to add a range of useful accessories later? Who can I ask for some useful, informed advice? Have I read as much about cameras as I should? Is there anything I need to ask the dealer before buying? The answers to these questions could help you avoid making the wrong purchase.

Look for a test report One way of finding out how a camera you are interested in performs is to read a test report. Many photographic magazines test the popular brands of camera, commenting on performance, specification, handling, and so on. Reading such a report beforehand can give you an impression of what to expect – but remember, it is *your* opinion that should decide the final purchase.

Your own trial run Most photographers would prefer to try a camera before buying, but this is rarely possible. If you have a friend who has a model similar to the one you are thinking of buying, ask his opinion of it. You may even be able to borrow it for a trial run. If you are on friendly terms with a local camera dealer, he or she may allow you to run a roll of film through the camera before buying. Do a few test exposures, have the film processed and analyse the results.

Specialist dealers While cameras are available from various sources, most keen enthusiasts buy from specialist photographic stores. This is mainly because of the dealer's specialist knowledge of the subject and because good dealers will not only stock a range of accessories but can also offer reliable camera repair and film processing services.

Mail order Be careful when buying cameras by mail order. While this is a simple and convenient way of buying, particularly if there isn't a camera store nearby, it often involves buying 'blind'. Remember, if you are not satisfied with your purchase, most mail-order companies offer a money-back guarantee.

About guarantees Most cameras are supplied with the manufacturer's worldwide warranty. Read the guarantee very carefully so that you know exactly what is covered in case of a fault. If a shop sells a faulty product, the onus is on them to replace or repair it.

Buying secondhand If you are looking for a camera bargain, the secondhand market is worth considering. Some specialist dealers offer used stock for sale and there are also plenty of secondhand bargains to be found in the classified sections of magazines, or even in your local paper. There is always the risk, however, of buying a 'dud'; so, ask for a guarantee.

Checking used cameras External damage is usually obvious on a used camera, but you can also check for serious faults in the meter and shutter mechanisms without exposing film. Point the camera at a bright light, set a wide aperture and operate the shutter: you should hear the camera set a fast shutter speed. In dim conditions, and with a small aperture, an automatic camera will set a much longer exposure – you should hear the shutter open and close quite distinctly. Read the camera's instruction booklet, and confirm that all other functions work as they should.

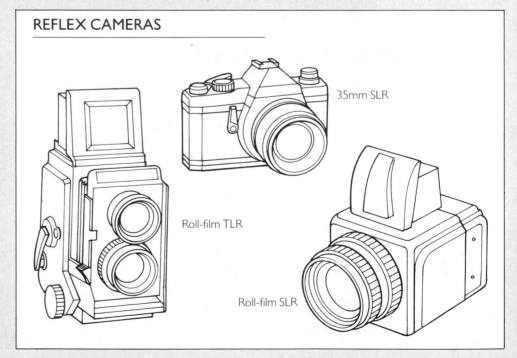

REFLEX CAMERAS

35mm SLR

Roll-film TLR

Roll-film SLR

35MM COMPACTS

For foolproof snapshot photography, 35mm compact cameras are hard to beat. On the newest models, virtually all camera functions are fully automated, so all the photographer needs to do is to point the camera and press the shutter release. Here are some points to look for when buying.

Autofocus Most of the more expensive compact cameras focus automatically, using a harmless infrared ray. When you press the shutter release, the camera's lens moves in towards the camera, focusing on progressively more and more distant subjects. Simultaneously, the infrared beam scans across the field of view until it falls on the subject in the centre of the picture. At this point, the camera 'knows' that the picture will be in focus, so the movement of the lens is arrested, and the picture is taken. All this happens in a fraction of a second, even in total darkness where manual focusing would be impossible.

Auto exposure All compact cameras set the exposure automatically. A photoelectric cell on the front of the camera measures subject brightness, and automatically sets the shutter speed and aperture to values that will yield a correctly exposed picture.

Film advance Virtually all compact cameras wind the film on to the next frame as soon as you've taken a picture, so there's no need to crank a lever wind or turn a wheel. Though the film is advanced quite slowly (about one picture a second) you can use this facility to take interesting sequences of pictures if you time your exposures carefully.

Rewinding Motorized cameras rewind the film for you when you reach the end of the roll. Some also allow you to rewind in mid-roll if you wish to get important pictures processed in a hurry. Though this facility prevents you from using the same

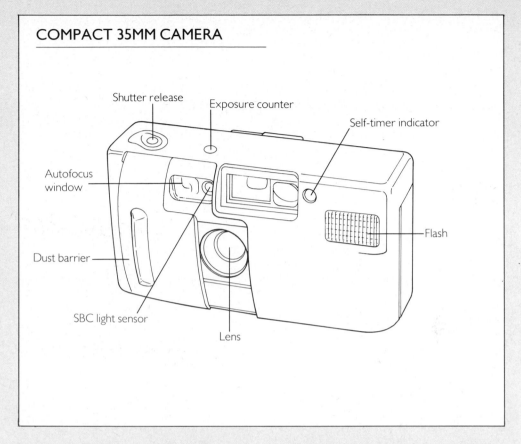

COMPACT 35MM CAMERA

Shutter release · Exposure counter · Self-timer indicator · Autofocus window · Dust barrier · SBC light sensor · Lens · Flash

film twice, it doesn't guard against you opening the camera in mid-roll – an error that even some seasoned professionals make from time to time. Older cameras may need manual rewinding – with these you press a button on the camera base, and turn the rewind crank until it rotates freely. Then you can take out the film.

Setting film speed The prominent chequered pattern on the 35mm cassette is the 'DX code' that contains information about the speed and type of the film. If your camera has the right contacts in the cassette chamber, it will automatically program the exposure meter with the correct film speed. The simplest cameras, which have only a single pair of contacts in the cassette chamber, can set only two speeds – ISO 100 and 400. If your camera is of this type, you should not use faster or

slower films. Other cameras can cope with a wider range of speeds. Cameras that are not equipped to read DX codes have a film speed dial that must be set manually to the ISO value printed prominently on the film carton.

Manual controls 35mm cameras are designed for effortless picture taking, so they lack most of the manual features that often confuse novice photographers. However, you may find a few simple controls that will help you compensate for non-average subjects. A backlight button gives extra exposure for subjects lit from behind, to prevent underexposure. For example, you'd need to press the button in when taking a portrait on a shaded hotel balcony – without compensation, the camera would be misled by the sunlit view behind, producing a silhouette.

Self timer Most compact cameras have a self-timer, to release the shutter after ten seconds delay, so that you can get yourself into the picture. You can use this feature in another way, too: if the camera is capable of giving long exposures in dim conditions (check the instructions) you can use the self-timer to take night-time pictures of static subjects. Just prop the camera up steadily, frame the subject, and operate the self-timer. The shutter will then open a few seconds later, and stay open until the film has had enough exposure. Operating the shutter in the normal way would jar the camera, so that movement would blur the picture.

Careful framing The viewfinder in most compacts is 'bright line' – that is, it gives a bright clear viewing image and features a line frame in which the picture should be composed. This is usually a bright yellow line which covers the outer edge of the viewfinder. When taking pictures, make sure any detail you require to include does not lie outside the line.

Compact flash A feature on many compacts is built-in electronic flash. On some cameras this needs to be switched on when indoor or night-time shots are being taken. Sometimes the flash comes into effect automatically when there is insufficient light available for an acceptable result. A small 'flash needed' warning light may flash in the camera viewfinder if the facility is needed. Make sure you wait until the flash has charged before taking a shot – this usually takes only a few seconds. Full charge is indicated by a neon light on the camera.

Frame counter To keep track of the number of pictures taken, compacts feature a frame counter, usually on top of the camera, which runs from 1 up to 36. Once the film has been inserted and the back of the camera closed, wind the film on to the '1' mark for the first frame. A motorised film advance should do this automatically.

Film safety check A feature found in some compacts is a film safety indicator. This is usually on the top of the camera and shows that the film is loaded correctly. If the indicator is not visible, re-open the camera in the shade and check that the film end is inserted into the take-up spool correctly. Make sure the perforations in the film line-up with the sprockets near the take-up spool, otherwise the film will not advance properly.

Accessories Various accessories are available for 35mm compact cameras. These vary from simple lens accessories, such as filters, to close-up lens attachments, cable releases (used for firing the camera shutter without touching, and possibly shaking, the camera) and other useful devices.

Telephoto options The more expensive compact cameras feature a telephoto or zoom option. By pushing a button, you can change to a lens with a longer focal length, and thus close in on the central portion of the subject. This is a valuable feature in situations where a closer approach to the subject is impossible – as in a zoo – but it adds considerably to the size and weight of the camera.

Data backs If you have difficulty identifying your pictures, you might appreciate a data back, which is an inexpensive optional accessory on most compact cameras. The data back imprints the date or the time in one corner of the picture, eliminating all uncertainty about when the photograph was taken. You can switch off the data imprint when you want to take a picture that would be spoiled by the inclusion of letters and numbers.

Don't spend more than you need Some compact cameras are highly sophisticated, but if you only want to take snapshots, advanced features may be a waste of money. As with any camera, don't buy facilities you're never likely to use.

POCKET CAMERAS

If you're on a beach holiday, even a 35mm 'compact' camera may seem like a burden. Disc and 110 cameras provide the answer. Both types are very much smaller than 35mm cameras, so they fit into even the tiniest beach bag.

Disc cameras These little cameras are little bigger than a pack of cigarettes. Instead of using a conventional strip of film, they take pictures on a circular disc of light-sensitive material. The principal advantage is compactness, and this is achieved at the expense of quality: though disc prints look fine at postcard size, they can't compare with pictures from 35mm film when enlarged to bigger sizes.

110 cameras 'Pocket instamatic' is another name for 110 format cameras. They take cartridges of film that simply drop into the camera, and rarely need any setting. The negatives are bigger than those on disc film, and picture quality is proportionately better. Some secondhand 110 cameras are remarkably sophisticated, though most current models offer only very basic facilities.

Obsolescence 110 and disc film formats have largely been superseded by compact 35mm cameras. Though you can still buy the cameras new and film is still available, it's worth bearing in mind that these cameras are essentially obsolete now, and repairs may become a problem.

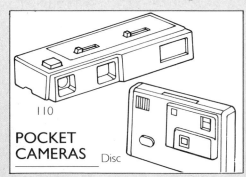

110

POCKET CAMERAS Disc

35MM SLR

Simple cameras are quite good enough for general photography but, if you want to be more creative, choose a 35mm SLR. This type of camera offers many useful facilities to help you take better pictures. With a SLR, you can add different lenses and other accessories, as well as make more effective use of exposure and focusing. SLRs vary from easy-to-use automatics through more sophisticated automatics to complex manual models.

Reflex viewing   When you look through the viewfinder of a 35mm SLR you see the subject through the actual picture-taking lens (viewing is through a separate lens system in simpler 'non-reflex' cameras). The subject is seen the right way up and the correct way round, i.e., there is no reversal of the image. This is achieved with mirrors. Light enters through the lens, is reflected up from a mirror through a focusing screen to a prism and comes out through the viewfinder.

Reflex advantages   The reflex viewing system has several virtues. Flexibility is the most obvious: SLR cameras are constructed so that you can remove the lens, and replace it with an optic that takes in more of the subject, or that enables you to enlarge a distant detail. Some non-reflex cameras have limited interchangeable lens capability, but only the SLR has such a wide range of interchangeable lenses.

Parallax   Another advantage of the SLR is that the subject appears in the viewfinder exactly as it will appear on film. If you photograph the sun just grazing the edge of a leaf, that's what your picture will show. By contrast, other types of camera suffer from 'parallax error' – in the viewfinder, you'd see the sun just touching the edge of the leaf, but on film, the leaf might completely hide the sun.

The reflex principle   Gently pressing the shutter release on an SLR initiates a complex sequence of events. First, the camera measures the light reflected from the subject, and judges which aperture and shutter speeds will yield correct exposure. Then a series of light sensitive cells in the base of the camera measure sharpness, and adjust the position of the lens until the picture is clear (see box). Further pressure on the shutter release then causes the reflex mirror to flip up, and the aperture to close down to the preselected value. Finally the shutter opens to expose the film. Then the mirror drops and the aperture opens to restore the image in the viewfinder (see below).

AUTOFOCUS SLR

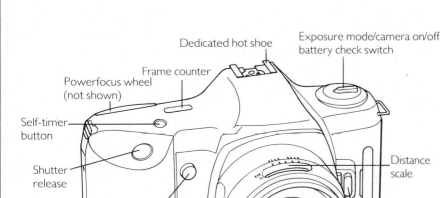

Dedicated hot shoe

Exposure mode/camera on/off battery check switch

Frame counter

Powerfocus wheel (not shown)

Self-timer button

Shutter release

Backlight button

Lens

Distance scale

Lens release button

THE REFLEX PRINCIPLE

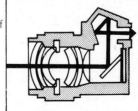

1. Light passes through lens to viewfinder via mirror and prism.

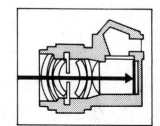

2. Shutter-release button pressed: mirror rises, aperture closes to required stop.

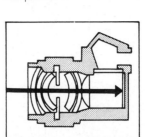

3. Shutter opens, exposing film immediately behind it.

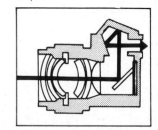

4. Shutter closes; aperture and mirror return to original positions.

HOW AUTO FOCUS WORKS

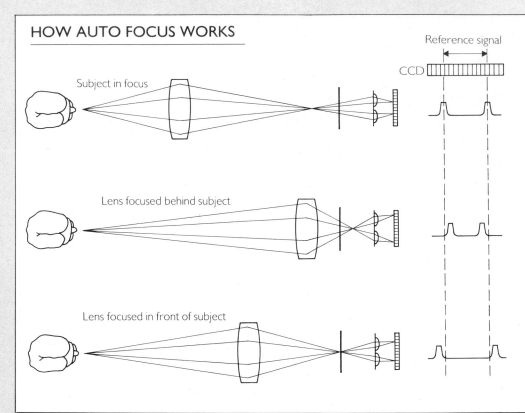

Reference signal

CCD

Subject in focus

Lens focused behind subject

Lens focused in front of subject

SLR cameras focus in a different way from compact 35mm cameras. Instead of projecting a beam of infrared, SLRs use a passive system – the camera examines the image of the subject, and moves the lens using a tiny motor until the picture is sharp. A portion of the main reflex mirror is semi-transparent, and the autofocus system 'steals' a little of the image from the lens, sending it down to a series of prisms and lenses below. Here, in a typical AF system, the image is split into two parts, each of which falls on an array of light-sensitive cells. The output from the cells is fed to the camera's microprocessor, which compares the pattern of the electrical 'peaks' with a pattern stored in camera's memory. When the two match, a signal lights in the viewfinder. All this happens so fast that you are hardly aware of it – the image snaps into focus in the viewfinder a split second after you press the shutter release.

When to focus manually The newest SLR cameras focus so effectively that you will rarely need to focus manually. However, autofocus systems always assume that the subject is central in the viewfinder, and if you're taking several pictures of off-centre subjects you will need to repeatedly turn the camera until the subject is central, half-press the shutter release, recompose the picture and press the shutter release. Manual focusing is often quicker, because you can focus just once.

Portraits with spectacles Autofocus systems 'home in' on hard-edged detail, so take special care when photographing people wearing glasses. For best results, the sharpest part of the picture should be the subjects' eye, but the camera may focus on the spectacle frame. Switch to manual if you frequently have this problem.

Prefocusing Autofocus systems often have problems maintaining sharp focus when the subject is rapidly approaching the camera. Here you may find it easier to switch off the autofocus system and use a technique known as prefocusing. Focus manually on a point through which the subject will pass as it approaches. Then wait until the subject has reached the chosen point before pressing the shutter release.

System SLRs The most sophisticated 35mm cameras are so-called system cameras. These differ from their humbler counterparts in ways that are subtle, but nevertheless crucial to the busy professional. The fundamental differences are ruggedness and modular construction: motor drive, viewfinder and camera back can all be interchanged to adapt the camera to specialist applications, and the cameras are designed to last a lifetime of heavy professional use. System cameras generally cost considerably more than run-of the mill SLRs, and frequently share the same lens system. So unless you have highly specialized needs, stick to a cheaper model.

SLR accessories the removable lens of an SLR makes fitting accessories very straightforward. For close-up photography, you can fit extension tubes or bellows between camera body and lens to enlarge the image on film. Using a short focal length lens, a bellows can magnify the subject 5 or 10 times, making spectacular pictures out of even mundane subjects.

Changing the viewfinder If you wear glasses and have difficulty seeing the whole of the SLR viewfinder, try fitting an eyesight correction lens over the view-finder window. You can then take your glasses off when focusing and composing the picture. Changing the camera's focusing screen for a different model can also help with manual focusing.

Inside the viewfinder Many camera adjustments can be made without taking your eye away from the viewfinder, thanks to the many indicating aids to be found in most modern SLRs. Apart from focusing aids there are often LEDs (light emitting diodes) showing exposure details, or even which direction to focus the lens. Older cameras feature a 'swing needle' indicating the lens aperture or shutter speed to select for a correct exposure.

ROLL-FILM SLR

If you are looking for more professional results, but wish to retain all the advantages offered by a reflex camera, consider a roll-film SLR. This type of camera uses 120 roll film, which offers a larger image area than 35mm (up to 6×6cm compared by the 2.4×3.6cm format of 35mm). Roll-film SLRs are much bulkier than 35mm cameras so, if you are considering one of these SLRs, handle it first. Hiring one from a specialist camera dealer for a short period may save you from making an expensive mistake (you will probably be asked for a returnable deposit).

Film format Roll-film cameras use 120 film (or the longer 220 film in some cases). A camera may offer one or more formats within this film size, including 6×6, 6×4.5, 6×7 and 6×9cm. Many professionals shoot on the square 6×6cm format so that their pictures can be easily cropped for reproduction in magazines. Most amateurs find the 6×4.5cm format a better shape, particularly for landscapes. The latter also provides you with more shots per film – 15 compared to 12 on the 6×6cm format.

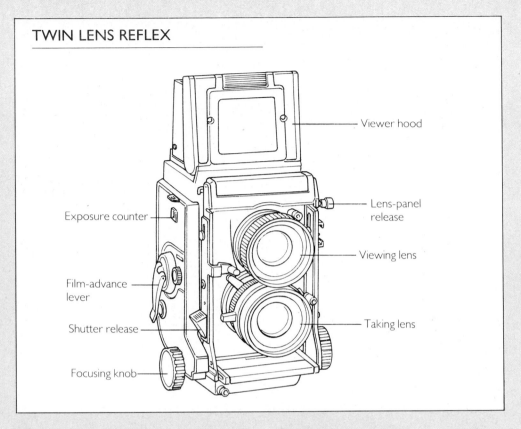

TWIN LENS REFLEX

- Viewer hood
- Lens-panel release
- Viewing lens
- Taking lens
- Exposure counter
- Film-advance lever
- Shutter release
- Focusing knob

Quality One major reason for choosing a roll-film SLR is the quality of the results. In many cases, an enlargement made from a 120 film negative can be of higher quality than one from a 35mm negative. Similarly many magazines prefer the size of 120 transparencies to 35mm because of their higher reproduction quality. If you know someone with a roll-film SLR, compare results with 35mm and judge for yourself. If you are happy with 35mm, you'd be well advised to stick with it.

Special backs Some roll-film SLRs feature interchangeable film backs. Such a facility is useful if you wish to carry a couple of ready-loaded film backs, or even change films (colour to black-and-white, for instance) during a shooting session. You can change format in some cases, or even switch films half-way through, using the remainder later if necessary.

Lenses and accessories As with 35mm SLRs, there is a wide selection of lenses and accessories available for roll-film cameras. Most roll-film SLRs require their own lenses, but certain accessories from your 35mm set-up may be used, e.g., tripods, filters, flash, and so on. However some accessories may have to be purchased specially, so bear this in mind when buying. Look carefully at the manufacturer's catalogue and see what items are available for the camera.

TLR cameras The twin lens reflex (or TLR) camera features separate viewing and 'taking' lenses. A single focusing control is used to operate both lenses together. The TLR uses 120 (or 220) film and offers many of the advantages of the roll-film SLR, but without parallax free viewing and, in some cases, the facility to change lenses or add useful accessories.

INSTANT PHOTOGRAPHY

Instant-picture cameras If you don't want to wait for your pictures to come back from the processors, one alternative is to buy an instant-picture camera. There are several types available and you can choose from simple point-and-shoot to more sophisticated models. In recent years instant-picture cameras and films have improved greatly, with much enhanced colour rendering, and improved permanence.

Instant film Most instant films are now of the 'integral' variety: the sensitive film layers and the processing chemicals are all enclosed between two sheets of plastic in a wafer-thin package. When you take a picture, the image from the lens exposes light-sensitive layers just beneath the surface of the transparent plastic cover sheet. As soon as the camera's shutter closes, an electric motor pushes the film through a kind of miniature mangle inside the camera. This ruptures a pod of processing chemicals, and the picture develops while you watch.

Film sizes and types There are several types of integral film, and you must buy the right one to fit in your camera. Other film types simply cannot be inserted into the film slot in the camera base. Don't be tempted to buy a Kodak instant camera even at bargain prices – Kodak instant film has been discontinued, and Polaroid packs do not fit.

Colour rendition For the best colour results, shoot in good, even light. Colour can look flat in dull lighting, but you can use flash to brighten up the subject outdoors if required. Bright props can help too, like clothing or an umbrella. Beware of bright sunlight which may cause the colours to appear very high in contrast – move the lighten/darken control to darker to prevent colours from appearing too 'bleached out' in strong lighting.

Using flash You can choose an instant picture camera with built-in flash (separate attachments are available for some models). Use flash indoors where there is insufficient light and outdoors to lighten-up a dull scene. The range of instant camera flash is usually limited, so shoot within 1.2-2.5 metres (4-8ft) for best results. You can avoid problems of 'red eye' by photographing the subject in a brighly lit area, or by asking the sitter to look away from the camera. If you use flashcubes or flashbars, keep some spares handy. Spare batteries (where required) for electronic flash are also a good idea.

Peel-apart film Besides integral films, Polaroid make several other types. Peel-apart films must be pulled manually from the camera after exposure, and the two sheets separated after a timed period of development. These films fit older cameras, and instant adapters for roll film SLRs.

Instant 35mm Most Polaroid films must be used in a special camera, but a few can be exposed in regular 35mm cameras. The most popular version produces instant colour slides: after exposing the whole film, you place it in a special processor with a pod of chemicals, and crank a handle to process the film. Other versions produce black and white slides, or high-contrast pictures.

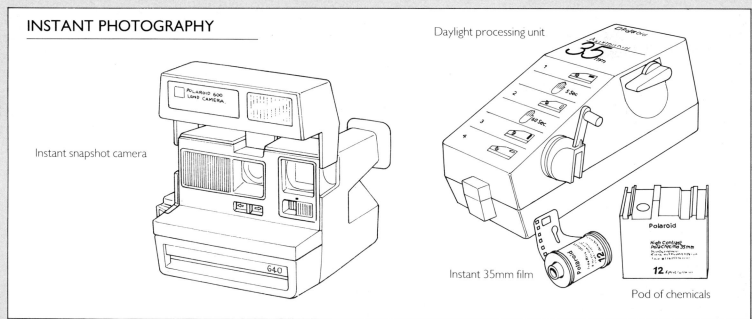

INSTANT PHOTOGRAPHY

Daylight processing unit

Instant snapshot camera

Instant 35mm film

Pod of chemicals

LENSES

UNDERSTANDING THE LENS

What is a lens? Lenses in all cameras, from the simplest 110 to the most complex roll-film model, are designed to do just one thing – to focus the image on the film. Light rays entering the camera are gathered together and sharply focused at the film surface.

Elementary Each lens is made up of one or more glass (or plastic) elements. A simple camera can have just one fixed element to focus the image. The standard 50mm lens on a 35mm camera might have a collection of six or seven different elements, all designed to direct and adjust the light, even improving image quality in some cases. These elements (or groups of them) move inside the lens housing when you focus.

Fixed lenses Most simple cameras have so-called 'fixed' lenses – these might be fixed mount and/or fixed focus. A fixed mount lens is there permanently – you can't replace it with another lens, as in some cameras. With a fixed-focus lens, the focusing range has been pre-determined by the manufacturer of the camera and you can't adjust it. Most shots should be reasonably sharp within a range of 2 metres (7ft) and infinity. To focus on a closer subject, you'll need to attach a supplementary close-up (see page 104).

Focus control Most photographers prefer to choose a camera with some kind of focusing control. This allows you to focus precisely on the subject within a certain distance range. The focus control (or ring) is located on the lens housing and rotates for focusing. If you can't usually focus through-the-lens (as on a 35mm reflex), guess how far the main subject is from the camera and set the focusing scale to that value (in feet or metres).

POPULAR LENSES

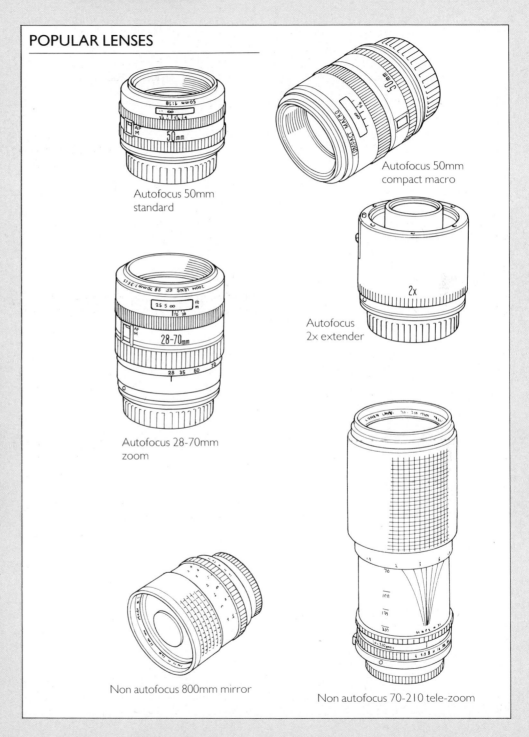

Autofocus 50mm standard

Autofocus 50mm compact macro

Autofocus 28-70mm zoom

Autofocus 2x extender

Non autofocus 800mm mirror

Non autofocus 70-210 tele-zoom

CHOOSING A LENS

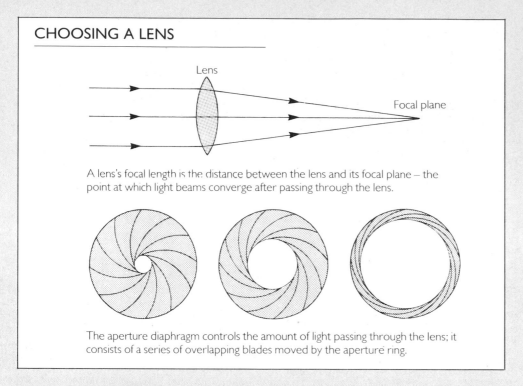

A lens's focal length is the distance between the lens and its focal plane – the point at which light beams converge after passing through the lens.

The aperture diaphragm controls the amount of light passing through the lens; it consists of a series of overlapping blades moved by the aperture ring.

Aperture and f-number The aperture numbers (f-numbers) engraved on the aperture ring indicate the size of the aperture only indirectly. Each number is really a ratio, representing the focal length of the lens, which is usually abbreviated to 'f', divided by the diameter of the aperture. This is why the f-number is often written f/4 or f/11. The advantage of this system is that all lenses let in the same amount of light when set to the same f-number – which wouldn't be true if the aperture ring was calibrated with the actual diameter of the aperture.

Aperture control The aperture control is one of two devices on the camera (the other is the shutter speed) for controlling the amount of light which reaches the film. When rotated, the control opens and closes a diaphragm inside the lens. This opens at stages called f/stops, marked on the control. The maximum aperture (or f/stop) of the lens is marked on the front, often in the form of a ratio such as 1:2.

Aperture range The range of f/stops can vary from lens to lens, typically, the range on a standard 50mm lens might be from f/16 to f/2.8. Remember that the smaller the f/stop number the wider the opening, so the maximum aperture of the lens might be f/2.8.

Longer focal length lenses usually have a more limited aperture range. A lens with a wide maximum aperture is described as being 'faster' than a lens with smaller maximum aperture e.g. an f/1.8 lens is 'faster' than an f/2.8. When comparing lenses, choose the fastest lens you can since the wider the maximum aperture, the easier it is to work in low light.

Zoom control Autofocus zooms usually have two simple controls: a broad ring for adjusting the focal length, and a narrow one for those rare occasions when manual focusing may be necessary. Manual zoom lenses fall into two categories: some have two rings just like an autofocus zoom, though the focusing ring is much wider.

These lenses are called 'two-touch' zooms. One touch lenses have a single ring, which you rotate to focus, and slide up and down the barrel to change the focal lengths.

Zoom creep If you are buying a one-touch zoom, try holding it vertically – the zoom collar must not 'creep' slowly down the barrel, as this alters the focal length.

Depth of field The area of sharpness in front of, and behind, the subject in focus varies when the aperture is changed. This is called depth of field. The smaller the aperture, the greater the depth of field, i.e., the area of sharpness is greater at f/16 than at f/2.8. If you want your subject and the background sharp, use a small aperture (f/16). If you want the background out of focus, use a large aperture (f/2.8). If in doubt, choose an aperture in the middle of the range (say, f/8).

Automatic diaphragm On an SLR all viewing and focusing is done at the fullest (and brightest) lens aperture, even when the aperture control is rotated. At the moment of exposure, the lens aperture closes-down to the f/stop set on the aperture control.

CHOOSING A LENS

Test reports One way to check the quality of a lens before you buy is to read a magazine test report. If you cannot find a report in a current issue, but a test has been done, the magazine can usually supply a copy or reprint. Just write in and ask. A charge may be made, but it can save you from making a costly mistake when choosing a lens.

The standard lens When you buy a camera it either has a fixed standard lens, or a separate standard lens is supplied to fit onto the camera. A standard lens is designed to give a 'normal eye-view' image of the subject. Remember that the focal length of a standard lens varies between some types of camera, relating to the size of the film format. Choose a 50/55mm standard lens for a 35mm SLR and an 80/85mm standard lens for a roll-film SLR. Most fixed lenses in 35mm compact cameras are slightly wider than standard, at around 38mm, to allow a slightly wider angle of view.

Additional lenses With an SLR you can choose lenses in addition (or even instead of) the standard lens. Select from wide angle, telephoto, zoom and other specialist lenses. But bear in mind that there are more lenses available than you can practically use – so be careful in choosing the lenses that you really need. Having a variety of lenses is only useful if they fit in with your particular requirements. Money spent on an unused lens would be better spent on a more useful accessory, or on film.

Wide-angle subjects Use a wide-angle lens for interior shots, when you need to include most of a room in the picture, but only have a limited amount of space available. You can choose a wide angle for photographing groups of people, for landscapes, or in other situations where a large expanse needs to be included in the shot.

Wide choice For most 35mm photographers, the wide angle choice is between either a 24 or 28mm lens. The former gives a slightly wider angle of view and may be handy for certain shots, but the 28mm is perhaps the more useful, and cheaper. The maximum aperture of the wide angle is also a factor – the difference between a 28mm f/2 lens and a 28mm f/2.8 can be as much as £100, but you would seldom use the extra stop provided by the f/2 lens.

Tele subjects Select the telephoto lens to match your subject. If you shoot portraits, a short telephoto (say, 105mm)

is possibly the most useful choice. For shooting sport or other action which takes place some way from your camera position, choose a longer telephoto (200mm upwards).

If you are trying to bring distant subjects closer, try a telephoto lens. The telephoto acts like a short telescope and allows you to photograph far away objects without the need to move in close with the camera. Tele lenses are longer in focal length than the standard lens – if 50mm is standard, then 135mm is typical for a telephoto lens.

Tele choice There is a good range of telephoto lenses for most 35mm cameras. Remember, the longer the focal length of the telephoto, the more it enlarges the subject. You may need a selection of different telephotos in your system. With a 35mm camera, consider a 135mm or 150mm lens first, then a longer 200 or 250mm lens, and possibly a 300 or 400mm for really distant work.

Zoom lenses A zoom lens is one which features an adjustable focal length over some fixed range such as 80-200mm. You can select any focal length within the range by moving the zoom control. This is obviously a big advantage over a conventional 'fixed' lens, and some zooms offer the equivalent of three or four 'fixed' lenses in one lens. One disadvantage is that very long focal length zooms can be heavy and difficult to handle.

Wide zoom For more versatile wide angle-shots, a wide zoom is a good choice. Most wide zooms start at around 24 or 28mm, extending to around 75 or 80mm at the other end of the focal length range. Because of this versatility, many photographers choose a wide zoom *instead* of a standard lens – the zoom can be used at the standard 50mm length, with the added facility of wider and longer zooming, so that the frame can be filled with bigger or smaller subjects.

Medium zoom For most subjects, a medium range zoom is probably most useful. Popular choices in this range are around 70-150mm. The wider end of the zoom range is just beyond standard lens length and is ideal for most close-in photography. At the longer end of the zoom range you can photograph distant subjects, or zoom in for portraits.

Long zoom If you continually photograph distant subjects (for example wildlife or sport) then a long zoom is a useful choice. Most long zooms start at around 200mm, extending to 600mm in some cases. Because of the long range this zoom is only worthwhile if needed for a subject that you photograph regularly.

Mirror lenses A mirror (or catadioptric or 'cat') lens is basically a compactly designed telephoto lens. Instead of the light entering the lens travelling straight from one end to the other through glass elements (as in a conventional tele lens) a system of mirrors inside the 'cat' lens reflects the light. This enables a long focal length to be achieved within a shorter and more compact lens. Because of the design the mirror lens does not have a diaphragm and, consequently, no aperture control. Light entering the lens is controlled by special filters.

'Macro' zooms To photograph really close-up detail you can buy a special macro lens. However, some zoom lenses offer a 'macro' facility which does allow you to move closer.

Macro lenses Buy a special macro lens for really close-up photography. A 50mm macro lens is offered as an alternative standard lens by some 35mm SLR manufacturers. A macro lens offers good quality, but usually at a hefty price. Macro zoom lenses have an extra close-up focusing facility. Don't buy a lens like this without first considering a zoom lens with a 'macro' facility or using close-up lens accessories.

In perspective When shooting buildings or examples of architecture, you will find when you tilt the camera upwards the verticals in the picture converge. To put this right, use a perspective control or 'shift' lens, whose lens elements can be moved to straighten converging lines. This lens is very expensive and should be considered only by the keenest amateur. For a one-off picture hire one if you really need it.

LENS ACCESSORIES

Teleconverters The cost of lenses is considerable – particularly long focal lengths, and for occasional telephoto shots you may prefer to fit an inexpensive teleconverter between the camera body and main lens. This multiplies the focal length, usually by 1.4× or 2×. There are drawbacks – the aperture of the lens falls in proportion to the magnification, and picture sharpness drops, too.

IN CLOSE

Close-up lenses You can increase the magnification of your lens for close-up work by fitting a close-up lens. This simply screws onto the front of the camera (choose the size to fit your lens filter thread) and allows close-ups at fixed, or varying, magnification, depending on the type of close-up lens. Use smaller apertures with such a lens to avoid blurred edges on your pictures (f/16 or f/11 should be about right).

Extension tubes The further away the lens is extended from the camera, the closer you can take pictures. You can buy a set of extension tubes (usually three per set) which fit between the camera and lens for close-up work. You can fit one or more tubes depending on how close you wish to photograph. Because the tubes contain no lens elements there is no optical interference with image quality.

Bellows extension The bellows extension works on the same principle as extension tubes, except that the bellows are adjustable and thus the magnifications can be altered – tubes are fixed and cannot be adjusted. When choosing bellows or tubes try and choose those with automatic coupling between camera and lens – this saves setting the aperture manually each time you take a shot. Bellows are easy to adjust but require firm support. And make sure you tighten the adjustment control each time, otherwise the shot may slip out of focus.

Reversing rings For taking close-up pictures one of the simplest methods is to put your standard lens into the camera the wrong way round for greater image magnification. The lens is attached to the camera via a reversing ring, which screws into the lens filter thread and the camera body. Before you buy a ring the close-up effect can be seen by holding the lens over the camera the wrong way round. With the lens reversed, the coupling for control of the aperture is lost, so set f/stops manually before each exposure.

Microscope For extreme close-up photography the camera can be fitted to a microscope eyepiece using a special adaptor. In some microscopes a separate optical system is used for the camera, allowing you to view through the microscope in the normal way.

Fish-eye effect Ultra wide-angle 'fish-eye' lenses are expensive to buy, but you can create fish-eye effects using simple

FILTER SYSTEMS

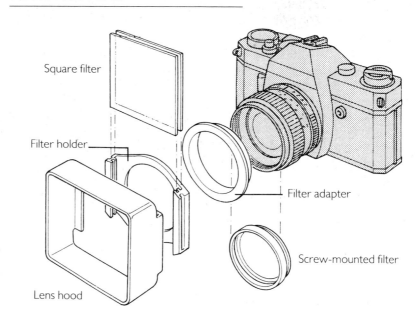

Square filter

Filter holder

Filter adapter

Lens hood

Screw-mounted filter

System filters fit onto the lens via a special holder and an adapter ring. This is a specially economical system if you use lenses with different sizes of filter threads, because a single set of filters will fit all the lenses. Most system filters are rectangular, and can slide within the holder – so that, for example, you can align the transitional area of a graduated filter with the horizon.

accessories. (Fish-eye lenses are so called because they make straight lines in the subject bulge outwards like a fish's vision.) You can buy a fish-eye attachment which screws onto the camera and costs a fraction of the price of a fish-eye lens. Or you can make your own fish-eye attachment by cutting a hole in a spare lens cap and fitting one of those wide-angle door 'spy' viewers. With the cap over your standard lens you can shoot fish-eye effects easily.

FILTER FACTS

Filter thread   You can buy a number of different filters for creating special effects, altering colour or contrast, and other uses. The circular type of filter is screwed into a special thread on the front end of the lens. Check when you buy the lens what the screw thread size is (say, 49mm) and, ideally, buy filters to fit. Don't worry if you have a number of different lenses with varying filter thread sizes. You can buy step-up or step-down rings which allow you to fit the same size filter to different filter threads.

Circular filters   These filters are probably the most widely used, and are available in varying sizes to fit most lenses. Most are made of glass and you should take care when handling them. You can use step-up or step-down rings to fit filters to different lenses, but some larger lenses may require their own filters, which can lead to expensive duplication, so bear this in mind when opting for filters of this type.

Square filter systems   If you intend collecting a set of lenses, consider buying a square filter system. This usually consists of a universal filter holder (which can be adapted to fit most lenses via a screw-in ring) and square filters which slot easily into the holder. This type of system is very flexible in that you can change the

filter quickly without removing the holder and the holder can be matched with most of your lenses. You can start with one filter and build your collection as required.

Filters for black-and-white   Don't just choose filters for colour photography – they can be just as important in black-and-white work. Because black-and-white films record colour as tones of grey, it is sometimes desirable to change these tones to achieve the best effect. This might involve bringing out the white clouds in a sky shot, or emphasizing foliage in a landscape, for example. By using a particular coloured filter (red, orange, yellow, blue, etc.) you can make these tonal changes quite easily. The chart below shows which filter colour to choose for specific shots.

FILTER CHOICE FOR BLACK-AND-WHITE PHOTOGRAPHY

Subject requirement	Filter colour
Whiten clouds in blue sky	Yellow
Darken sky dramatically	Red
Lighten foliage in scene	Green
Lighten blue sky, losing cloud shapes	Blue

Filter strength   The various coloured filters for monochrome work are available in different strengths (or densities) to match individual picture requirements. A 1X red filter, for instance, would be less powerful (and provide less effect) than a 2X red filter. Use a 1X if in doubt – the density of the image can always be increased later, at the printing stage.

Colour-correction filters   Most colour slide film is balanced for shooting in average daylight conditions. Shoot indoors under artificial lamplight, or outdoors late in the day, and the results may look too orange or 'warm'. To 'cool down' the colour for a more natural colour balance you need a blue 80A colour-correction filter. Similarly if you use a colour film

balanced for lamplight (tungsten) in daylight, the over-blue results need to be 'warmed up' by using an orange 85B colour-correction filter. You will also need to filter a daylight film shot under fluorescent light, which can produce a green tinge on the film. The chart below gives the correct filter to use.

COLOUR-CORRECTION FILTERS

Film in use	Shooting situation	Filter choice
Daylight	Indoor lamplight	Blue (80A)
Tungsten	Normal daylight	Orange (85B)
Daylight	Under fluorescent lights	FL/D

Special-effects filters   While there are many special-effects filters available (see pages 37-40), use one only if the picture really needs it. Filters can improve many pictures, but they can also ruin them. A wrongly used filter can often obstruct the real objective of the photograph.

Other useful filters   Two standard filters used by many photographers are the skylight 1A and the polariser. The skylight can be kept over the lens permanently and is useful for absorbing ultra-violet 'haze' in landscape scenes, resulting in clearer images. The Polariser can be used to minimise reflections when photographing glass or water, as well as making a blue sky much deeper in colour shots.

Soft effect   It is possible to buy a 'soft focus' effect filter which will create a misty result around the edges (for portraits, etc.) However it can be done more cheaply (and more accurately) by smearing Vaseline around the edges of a skylight filter. The effect can be varied and the smear can be wiped off later with a lens-cleaning cloth. Do not smear the lens itself otherwise it may be permanently marked.

EQUIPMENT

CHOOSING A FLASH

Built-in flash Many simpler cameras and 35mm compacts have built-in flash. This facility means there is one major accessory you don't have to worry about. Of all the accessories available, flash is perhaps the most useful, even vital, in poor light or indoor situations. Consider choosing a camera with this useful facility when shopping around.

Buying a flashgun There is a huge choice of portable flashguns on the market and selecting the right one can be daunting. Just remember that all you are buying is a portable light source and that this must be compatible with your camera. Make sure it can provide the light output you require and is straightforward to operate.

Power output The light output of a flashgun is usually indicated by its Guide Number (GN). The higher the GN, the more powerful the flash. The GN can also be used to calculate exposure required for a correct flash exposure, but most of today's automatic flash units calculate exposure automatically.

Portable power Most flash units are powered by AA-size penlight batteries or by AC mains via a small optional adaptor. Some also accept rechargeable NiCad (Nickel Cadmium) cells which are expensive to buy initially but can work out cheaper than continually replacing conventional batteries, though of course you will need a battery charger. Some larger flash units require a portable power pack which can be recharged before use.

Manual flash This is the simplest form of flashgun. Each time it is fired, the full light output of the unit is discharged. This means you cannot just add a touch of flash light to the subject (as with an automatic unit) and the batteries are drained much more quickly. However most manuals are cheaper than the automatics – it is possible to buy a small manual for under £10.

Automatic computerised flash Most modern flash units now feature computer thyristor circuitry to control light output. An automatic unit can produce exactly the right amount of light for the subject. When the flash is fired, a sensor on the front of the unit measures the light reflected by the subject and 'cuts off' the light output to give a correct exposure. An auto unit is the best choice for most types of photography.

X-sync and hot shoe When you plan to use an electronic flashgun with any camera, make sure that it is connected for synchronization. Most cameras, particularly 35mm SLRs, feature a hot shoe on the top plate. This provides direct electrical contact, automatically firing the flash when it is attached and avoiding the need for a connecting cable. If there is no hot shoe on your camera, connect the lead from the flash to the X-sync (synchronization) socket on the camera. SLRs have a maximum shutter speed for flash sync 1/60 or 1/125 second; do not exceed it or only part exposures will result.

Zoom head When taking flash pictures with telephoto or zoom lenses, you need a unit with a longer and narrower light throw. So look for a unit with a zoom control, which can be adjusted from normal flash output to longer throw by simply extending a special magnifying lens on the front. The amount of extension is usually numbered to be compatible with a particular lens focal length.

Twin tube When you take pictures of someone by bouncing flash light off a ceiling, the effect can be rather 'flat' and you can end up with awkward face shadows. To counter this problem, some flash manufacturers offer units with a twin tube. The large main tube can be directed upwards for bounced light, with a second smaller tube facing directly at the subject.

Flash accessories It is possible to buy special accessories to fit many flashguns. Coloured filters fitted over the flash tube can create special lighting effects. You can also buy diffusers which 'soften' the light produced by the unit, for a less harsh result in a portrait, for instance. Extension leads can be used to hold the flash away from the camera when trying out different directions for the lighting.

Dedicated flash Today's SLR cameras have 'dedicated' flash units. These flash guns automate flash photography, and features vary from unit to unit. Most set

FLASH UNITS

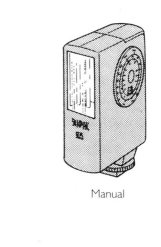

Manual

the camera to the correct shutter speed; some meter the flash through the camera's lens; many illuminate a 'flash recycled' light in the camera's viewfinder. And newer models have an infrared light source so the camera can focus in the dark.

Flash slave If you are using more than one flashgun at a time, to provide lighting from a variety of angles, the units don't all have to be connected up to the camera for synchronization. Just connect one unit to the camera and fit a flash 'slave' to each of the other units. This is a tiny photoelectric cell which senses light from the main flashgun and automatically fires the unit it is attached to at the same time.

Ring flash For very close-up photography it can be difficult to light the subject with the lens so close to it. If you are likely to do much close-up work, consider buying a ring flash. This is a circular flash tube which fits around the front of the lens, and, in effect, takes the flash in as close as the lens, virtually eliminating the shadows that often mar close-ups.

Infrared flash There. are situations – when photographing animals at night, for instance – when you need to take flash shots without the flash being seen. An infrared flashgun emits infrared light which cannot be seen by the naked eye. But, used in conjunction with infrared film, well-lit images can be produced – without the subject knowing anything about it. Infrared flashguns are fairly expensive, but infrared film costs little more than standard film.

LIGHTING ACCESSORIES

Coloured filters When working with studio lights you can change colour and tone by adding filters to your camera (see pages 104-105), or by putting filters over the lighting. You can buy large gelatin filter squares to cover one or more lights. This is particularly useful if you want to make a background a particular colour without affecting the light in the foreground (a lens filter would make the whole scene the same colour).

Umbrellas Direct flash light can be quite harsh, particularly with some of the stronger types of studio flash. To soften the light, you can attach a reflector umbrella onto the lighting stand. Turn the light source to face into the umbrella (not at the subject) so that the light reflects from the inside of the 'brolly', giving a softer light overall. Umbrellas are commonly used for most types of studio photography, but particularly for portraits. They come in white, silver or gold – white for most uses, silver for a 'harder' effect, gold for a 'warmer' effect, e.g. in colour portraiture.

Diffusers You can soften the light without deflecting it from the subject by using a diffuser. This consists of semi-transparent white gauze material, which fits over the front of the flash and disperses the light in a wider direction for a less intense effect or for use with a wide angle lens. You can improvise your own diffuser from tracing paper.

Reflectors Because lighting is very directional some parts of the subject may be unlit, or in shadow. To fill these areas you can use another light source, but a cheaper alternative is to use a reflector. You can buy reflector squares (white or silver), but any bright reflective surface (even an old white sheet) will do the job, placed on the opposite side to the flash, and to the side of the subject. Extra light will be reflected into the darker areas for a more balanced result.

Tungsten lighting You don't have to use flash in the studio. Ordinary tungsten or photoflood lamps can be used. You can buy special lighting stands with fittings for large photoflood bulbs. This type of lighting is easy to use, but you will have to use slide film balanced for this lighting when using colour or use colour-correction filters. Don't be tempted to use the more powerful photofloods in conventional lighting fitments for more than a few seconds, as they get very hot.

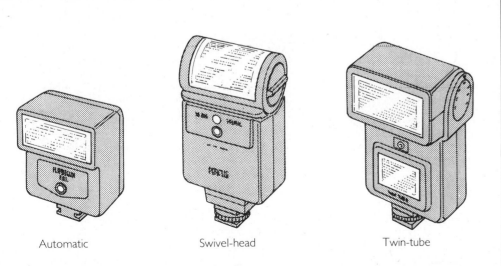

Automatic   Swivel-head   Twin-tube

Manual flash guns are basic and inexpensive, but automatic units are easier to use, and consume less battery power. A swivel head allows you to bounce flash from the ceiling for softer lighting; adding a second flash tube puts a sparkle in the portrait subject's eye, and improves modelling.

CAMERA SUPPORTS

Tripods Of all the different camera supports, the tripod can provide the most flexible range of adjustment. Most tripods are made in light aluminium and are therefore easy to carry, yet firm enough to support your camera. Various sizes are available so, when buying, extend the legs and supporting arm of each type to see which is best for your requirements. Check that the legs lock into place firmly.

Pan-and-tilt head This type of head has a single arm which you use to tilt the camera up and down and from right to left. Turning the arm locks the camera angle in position and it can then be loosened when you need to change the shooting angle.

Reversible head On many tripods the legs cannot be set for very low angle shots. Some types, however, allow you to remove the centre support holding the camera and insert it upside down, which can enable you to shoot right down to ground level. You may have to shoot through the gaps between the tripod legs, so bear this in mind when using a wide-angle lens, which might include the legs in the view.

Rifle grip This is used for shooting pictures, rather than bullets. This extending arm of the support is ideal for camera-and-long-lens combinations and the grip is strapped to one shoulder for extra support. A cable release is fitted to the grip's triggering device for firing the camera shutter. Such a grip is ideal for fast-action photography.

SPECIAL RELEASE AIDS

Cable release One of the hazards of taking pictures is camera shake, when the camera moves slightly during an exposure. The result is often a blurred picture. You can avoid touching the camera at the moment of exposure by attaching a cable release to the shutter release button.

Longer cable releases Conventional cable releases are literally made from a flexible cable sliding inside a tube, and friction puts a limit on the length. Modern cameras, though, have shutter releases that can be operated by an electrical flex, and this can be much longer. Long cable releases are valuable for self portraits, because you can time the exposure when you choose.

CAMERA SUPPORTS

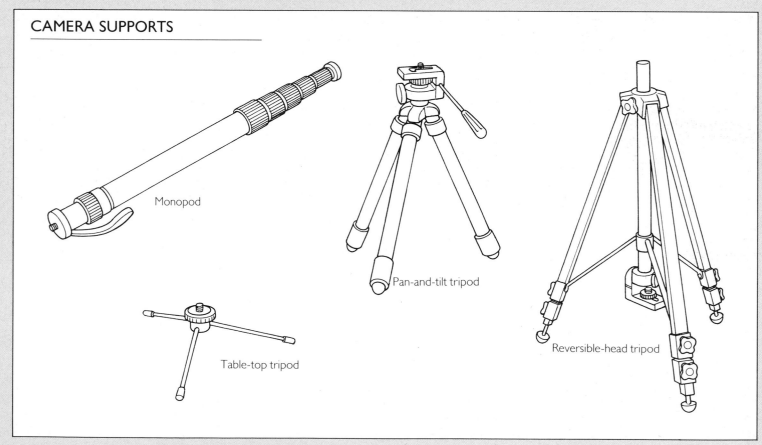

Monopod

Table-top tripod

Pan-and-tilt tripod

Reversible-head tripod

Air releases If you wish to operate a mechanical camera from a distance, buy an air release. This operates the shutter with a piston, at the end of an airtight tube. Squeezing a bulb at the other end operates the shutter.

Infrared release If you want to fire the camera from a distance (say, for certain types of wildlife photography where the photographer can hide away from the camera position) try an infrared release. This works on a similar principle to some TV remote control units. An infrared beam is emitted by the hand control to a compatible unit on the camera which fires the shutter. If the camera is also fitted with a motorized film winder, you can shoot a number of pictures continuously (otherwise you would have to keep going back to the camera to wind on the film after each frame had been exposed).

MISCELLANEOUS AIDS

Hand-held meters Many professional photographers prefer not to rely on their camera's TTL meter, and instead measure light with a hand-held meter. These meters can measure incident light – the light falling on the subject, rather than that reflected from it. They therefore provide a more accurate indication of exposure with very dark or light subjects which can easily mislead a built-in meter.

Spot meter An ordinary hand-held light meter will normally provide a very general reading of the whole scene being photographed. But there are some situations where you may wish to record the light level in only one part of the scene, or the different areas of light and dark in a shot. For this, use a spot meter which has a very narrow measuring angle and can be used to measure any small area of the subject.

Data backs When shooting many photographs at once, you might want to

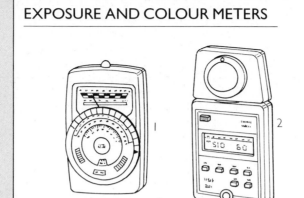

EXPOSURE AND COLOUR METERS

A hand-held exposure meter (1) increases exposure precision, especially with difficult subjects and transparency film. Negative film is more tolerant of exposure errors, so your camera's TTL meter usually provides sufficient precision. Colour meters (2) can be used to match film to light source, and thus prevent colour casts in unusual light.

keep a record of when they were taken, exposure details, or other information. In many cases you can simply write this down when shooting, but an alternative is to use a data back to replace the conventional back on your 35mm camera. The dials on the data back can be preset for any specific numerical information (time, date, frame number, etc.) and this information will automatically be transferred onto the margin of the film when you shoot each exposure. The figures will appear at the bottom of the frame. The data back is battery driven, and can be switched off if you don't wish to have any information on a particular frame of film.

Bulk film backs If you use conventional prepacked 35mm film cassettes, the maximum number of exposures you can shoot is 36 with most films. You can increase this considerably by fitting a bulk film back to your SLR. This back accommodates larger rolls of bulk film, which you can buy and load yourself to a required length, which may be up to 30 metres (100ft). A bulk film back is useful for covering events where a large number of pictures need to be taken quickly – a sports event, for example.

Interchangeable backs On many roll film SLRs you can change the film back

(even in mid-film) to shoot on another type of film. For example, a switch from black and white to colour is possible.

Motorized film advance The majority of new cameras have some sort of motorized film advance built in. These advance the film immediately after exposure, so you need never miss a picture. Some can be set for continuous operation – as long as you keep the shutter release pressed in, the camera will continue to take pictures until the film runs out. Continuous shooting doesn't guarantee that you'll catch the best moment in a rapidly-changing scene – you're more likely to get a good picture if you bide your time and take just a couple of pictures at exactly the right moment.

High-speed motor drives For sports and action photography, the motorized film advance built into regular SLRs is just too slow, so professional system cameras have a separate 'bolt-on' motordrive, with only manual advance as standard. These drives may advance the film as fast as 5 frames per second, and often also feature a control to allow you to shoot a preselected number of frames. All high-speed motor drives can rewind the film at the end of the roll. Though this may seem an unnecessary luxury, it can save valuable seconds when you're under pressure.

FILM

FILM BASICS

Film speeds Every film is designed to respond to a range of lighting conditions and this range is denoted in ISO figures on the film or film carton. Generally speaking, the lower the ISO figure, the better the light conditions should be when using it. For example a film like Kodachrome 25 slide film should really be used only in bright conditions. For very low light, you might need a film rated at around ISO 1000. Most popular colour negative/print films are rated at ISO 100, which is a central rating, usually producing acceptable results in reasonable lighting conditions.

Film storage Film should be kept in a cool, damp-free place. Storage in a refrigerator is recommended for some colour films. Some films need to be kept in a freezer for long-term storage, but check with the manufacturer's instructions first.

Film markings When a film has been processed, you can see a variety of different markings on the negatives. Each negative should be numbered to enable reprints to be ordered later and this is the only mark which need concern you.

COLOUR NEGATIVE/PRINT FILM

How it works The most popular type of film in use is colour negative/print film. If you want colour prints, you can choose one of these films. When the film is processed you have a set of colour negatives from which your prints are made.

Popular speeds Most colour neg film is available in ISO 100 rating and this is fine for the vast majority of shooting situations. However, if you are likely to be shooting in lower light or bad weather conditions, consider one of the faster films. Kodak, for instance, offer colour neg films rated at ISO 100, 200, 400 and 1000 – a range which should cover most situations.

High resolution Recent developments in film technology have produced so-called 'high resolution', or HR, films. Because of the way the HR film emulsion is made, it is possible to achieve much sharper and more colourful results on these films. It probably won't be long before all colour neg films feature the HR emulsion, and they are certainly the best choice for the enthusiastic photographer who is looking for the sharpest possible quality.

Exposing colour negatives Accuracy of exposure is important for best results with all types of film. But there is a reasonable amount of tolerance with colour neg film. If you under- or over-expose the film this can usually be corrected at the printing stage. Automatic printing machines at a processing laboratory can usually produce an acceptable result from a wrongly-exposed colour negative. Some photographers deliberately over-expose the film (by one or two f/stops) for a stronger colour effect. Remember that colours can look muddy if the film is under-exposed.

Colour negative economies Prints made at the time of film processing are always very much cheaper than reprints. So if you think you may want two copies of several pictures on a roll of film, you can save money by asking for processing and two sets of prints. Similarly, 'custom' prints which crop out unwanted detail are more costly than an enlargement from the full frame. If you want a picture cropped, it is much cheaper to order a larger full-frame print, and trim off the bits you don't need.

COLOUR SLIDE FILM

How it works Colour slide film is also known as colour transparency, or reversal, film. The latter name is probably most descriptive because, when you shoot pictures on this type of film, the result is not a negative (from which you would make a positive print image) but a reverse negative, i.e., a *positive* image. So you end up with the colours as seen in the subject.

Film choice Colour slide films are available in various sizes and types. Within all the various makes, there are two basic types of slide film – *substantive* and *non-substantive*. Substantive films contain colour dyes in the emulsion and can be processed by a laboratory of your choice, or at home (see Darkroom chapter). With non-substantive films, like Kodachrome 64, dyes are introduced at the processing stage and so the films must be returned to the manufacturer for processing. With non-substantive films, such as Kodachrome 64, the cost of the film includes processing by the manufacturer.

Popular speeds There is no fixed standard speed for slide film. One of the slowest slide films is Kodachrome 25, which offers very high quality results, but requires good lighting conditions. Kodak Ektachrome and similar films from manufacturers like Agfa are available in medium speed ISO 200, and even faster ISO 1600 for low-light work.

Film differences Slide films vary in the results they produce. This is often because they are made differently, but even those of similar type have their own characteristics. You can see differences even between Kodachrome and Ektachrome (both made by Kodak) because of their construction and the difference in processes used. Experiment by trying a few different types of film and keep a record of likes and dislikes for future reference. Some films may be more suitable for certain types of picture than others. Kodachrome 25, for example, is more suited to very bright and colourful subjects than a faster Ektachrome, which produces slightly softer hues.

Prints from slides It is possible to make prints from slides using special reversal paper like Cibachrome. A laboratory can do this for you (usually much more expensive than print from a negative) or you can print at home using a printing kit.

Slide 'pushing' As with Black and White film, you can increase the working ISO speed of slide film. For example, you can shoot a 200 ISO film at 400, then increase the development time at the processing stage for accurately exposed results. Most laboratories offer an uprating service for this purpose, but some make a small extra charge.

Instant slides To produce slides instantly use Polachrome instant-slide film. By means of a special hand-held processor (which can be used in normal light) the exposed film is developed, producing a roll of slides within minutes. This is useful for pictures which are needed very urgently. The results are not usually as good as conventional ·slide film, but they are acceptable.

BLACK-AND-WHITE FILM

How it works Conventional black-and-white film captures the colours we see not only in black-and-white, but in all the shades of grey in between. Most of the black-and-white photography we see is reproduced in newspapers, magazines, books, and so on. Many enthusiastic photographers recognize the individual qualities offered by black-and-white photography, such as its increased emph-

asis on texture and composition. Monochrome film also has a practical advantage: since it is essentially colour blind, you can dispense with filtration and still get good results in all manner of lighting conditions.

Film choice Black and white makes a refreshing change from colour film, but monochrome needs careful processing and printing to get good results. Unless you have your own darkroom, check that the local photo-lab can process the film for you. You may have to wait longer than for colour films, and the cost of processing may be higher.

Slow film For high quality results, a slow film (around ISO 50) is the best choice. With minimal grain, the negative produces a very fine image although it can be quite 'contrasty', i.e., with very deep blacks and bright whites. This contrast can be reduced in processing by reducing the development time. Slow film is ideal for portraits, copying work, or if very fine detail is required.

Medium-speed film The best film-for-all-occasions is a medium speed film of around ISO 125. This is fine enough for good quality results and fast enough for shooting in most conditions.

Fast film For low light work (bad weather, indoors, and so on) or situations where you need to use a fast shutter speed (sport, for instance) choose a fast film around the ISO 400 rating. This type of film produces slightly grainier results than slower films, but under difficult conditions, shooting on fast film is better than not getting the picture.

Chromogenic films Not all black-and-white film has a fixed ISO rating. The chromogenic films, such as Ilford XP1 or Agfa Vario XL, are designed for use at practically any ISO speed. You can start taking shots at an event at ISO 200, then

switch to 400 *on the same film* if the weather turns cloudy. No change to the processing cycle is needed, and all the shots will be printable. Choose a chromogenic film if you don't want to carry a variety of different films around. You can buy the films with their own special processing chemicals.

About grain Because black-and-white film is made up of silver halide 'grains' in the emulsion, this graininess can be seen in the processed negative and, consequently, the print. Remember that the faster the ISO speed of the film, the more grain it contains and the more visible this will be on the final image.

Home processing Most serious photographers choose to process their own black-and-white films at home because it is cheaper and more rewarding than laboratory processing. Providing there is space for a darkroom, home processing is within the abilities of most enthusiasts.

Contacting You can buy a special contact printer to hold negatives and paper together, or you can simply lay the negatives flat on the paper and cover with a sheet of clean glass. Expose under an enlarger lamp (or similar light source) and develop the print in the normal way. All the pictures can be assessed on the sheet and selections made for enlargement.

Push processing While black-and-white films generally have a fixed ISO speed rating, there may be occasions when you wish to increase the speed (perhaps to cope with bad light). Uprating film will increase the grain and contrast of the image, lowering its quality but often enhancing its atmosphere. If you decide to 'push' the speed of an ISO 400 film to ISO 800, increase the development time at the processing stage if you are doing your own processing or ask the laboratory to uprate the film. Details for 'push processing' are usually provided with your developer.

THE DARKROOM

DARKROOM LAYOUT

Bathroom This makes a good temporary darkroom, provided you arrange sessions to give least inconvenience to the rest of the family (late at night is probably best). At night a blind over the window can give adequate blackout. A good, firm board across the bath can be used for dishes, tanks and beakers, but the enlarger and other electricals, such as the safelight, must be kept well away from the wet area. If the board across the bath is edged to form a tray, a hose can carry spillage direct to the bath outlet, avoiding chemical staining.

Box room It may be ideal if there is a water supply, but for occasional use a bucket can be taken to and from a bathroom tap. Blackout screens can be constructed of ply, the edges backed with felt, and fitted tight with turnscrews to the window frame. A bench is more useful than a table, as an undershelf is handy for storage. Measure the bench space needed to take enlarger, dishes and so on, and plan the work surfaces accordingly. A bedroom screen can also be used to darken a corner if heavy curtains are drawn over the window.

Changing bag This is sometimes called

the smallest darkroom. Obtainable through dealers, a changing bag is usually a double-skinned square bag of black opaque material. There is a lightproof zipped entry for a developing tank, film, scissors, and elasticated sleeves which pull up over the wrists. Inside, you can easily draw a film from its cassette and load it into the tank, ready for processing. It is adequate for film processing, as all further stages can be carried out in normal light.

For black-and-white The loaded tank and beakers of developer, stopbath and fixer can be contained in a large dish to confine spillage. This can occupy part of

THE DARKROOM

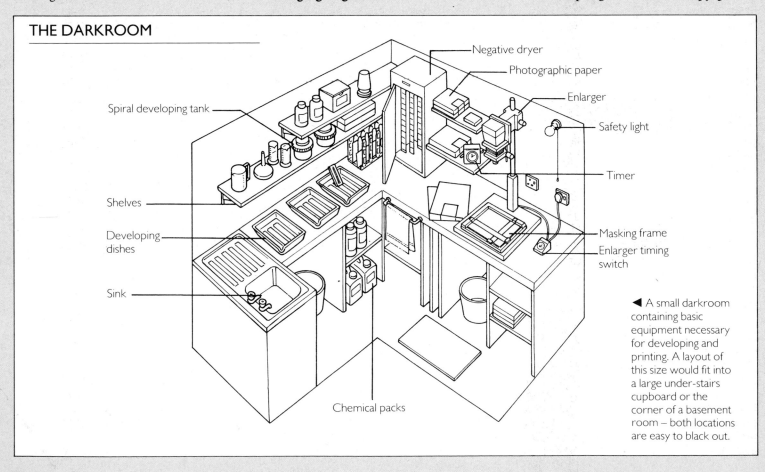

Negative dryer

Photographic paper

Enlarger

Safety light

Timer

Masking frame

Enlarger timing switch

Spiral developing tank

Shelves

Developing dishes

Sink

Chemical packs

◀ A small darkroom containing basic equipment necessary for developing and printing. A layout of this size would fit into a large under-stairs cupboard or the corner of a basement room – both locations are easy to black out.

the area normally used for three dishes when processing prints. Three 20×25cm (8×10in) dishes need about 90cm (3ft) of bench space. The average enlarger will occupy about 45×55cm (18×22in), but workspace alongside is needed for boxes of printing paper. Allow sufficient height above the bench for the enlarger head to be fully raised.

For colour printing Enlarger space is the same as for black-and-white, but colour processing is now done in a cylindrical drum, which occupies less space than is needed for dishes. An area 30×60cm (12×24in) is adequate. Total darkness is required for colour printing, and even a small chink of light can cause unwanted colour casts. However the drum used for processing is sealed against light, so after exposure in total darkness the paper can be processed in daylight.

For slides Although developing slide films calls for careful attention to detail, very little room is required. Darkness is needed only while loading the film into the tank, which can be carried out in a changing the bag. After that, subsequent developing processes are carried out in normal lighting.

Electricity If you have a room specially for the purpose, make sure you start out with sufficient plug points. For serious work, you may eventually need points for enlarger, timer, safelight, colour processor, film dryer, print dryer and heater.

Wet and dry Depending on the space available you should try to keep wet and dry areas separated, as in professional darkrooms. In a small area, this may be achieved simply by erecting a dividing board between the dry and wet ends of a single bench or table. There is usually the odd drop of spillage when transferring prints from dish to dish, and a divider prevents a splash reaching unprocessed, and expensive, paper.

Left to right Everyone has a way of working that comes easiest to them. Ideally, arrange the layout so that you work from enlarger to wet processes and then direct to the sink. Having the wet processes closest to the sink makes for easier mopping up. Whether your prints are air-dried in a rack or passed through a dryer, keep them well away from the sink after washing.

Storage This is often an afterthought in the amateur darkroom, but a little pre-planning leads to much happier usage. Dishes take up little space when stored upright in slots under the bench. Bottles of chemicals in use should be ready to hand on a shelf over the wet bench. A thermometer can rest in its case, if this is taped vertically to the wall near the processing area. Arrange shelves and hooks so that film clips, beakers, print dodgers and other items in constant use are ready to hand.

Comfort In designing a darkroom many amateurs forget the space they themselves occupy. Arrange bench height so that you can sit comfortably at the enlarger without crouching. About 71cm is right for most people.

SAFETY FACTORS

Ventilation Blacking out a room can make it almost airtight, which is dangerous to health. Some amateurs working in a confined space make do by opening and closing the door a few times every five minutes or so, which is effective but erratic. Dealers can supply a light-trapped ventilator, or a simple boxform ventilator can be made and installed in the door. This is matt black inside, with an opening at the top on the outside and at the bottom on the inside.

Chemicals Always read the instructions carefully. Some chemicals, such as

bleaches and toners, should never be mixed or used in a confined space, as their fumes may be poisonous. Some chemicals carry an irritant or poison warning, with advice in case of emergency. *Never* leave photographic chemicals within reach of small children.

Humidity The small darkroom is the worst place to keep your treasured albums of colour and black-and-white negatives, or boxes of slides. However well you clean up after use, there is probably more moisture in the air here than elsewhere in the house, and this can lead to mould on the emulsion. Take negatives into the darkroom only for a printing session; then remove them to a dry room.

A safety routine Don't just develop prints – develop a safety routine as well. After you have taken a sheet of paper from its packet or box, close the container immediately. There is nothing more irritating to a photographer than discovering, when he or she switches on the light to examine a print, that an expensive stock of unexposed paper has been ruined. If you are exposing several sheets of paper before processing, keep them in a closed box.

A lethal mixture Water and electricity don't mix. One plug per socket should be the rule. We know of an amateur who had a two-way bayonet adaptor hanging on a nail which came out of the wall, allowing the adaptor to fall into the dish of developer he had his hands in – until just one second before the lethal flash!

BLACK-AND-WHITE FILM

Equipment For black-and-white processing of film, you need only a tank and a thermometer. Extras are a set of beakers and a film wiper. The same beakers can be used for making up chemicals for processing black and white papers. For the latter, you will need a set of three dishes to hold developer, stopbath and fixer. Opaque or coloured bottles with good stoppers are useful for storing used solutions.

Chemicals When a picture is taken, the image on the film cannot be seen until it is 'revealed' or developed. This is the job of the developer. What it does, in fact, is to blacken the tiny grains of sensitive silver in the emulsion which have been affected by the image projected on the film by the lens. When sufficient developer action has taken place, the developer is poured out of the film tank and replaced with a stopbath, an acid solution which arrests the development process. Finally, the film is immersed in a fixer, so-called because it washes away the unexposed silver grains and 'fixes' the negative image. The film is then washed and dried.

Paper The light-sensitive emulsion of black-and-white printing paper is similar to that of the film, but slower acting. It is composed mainly of light-sensitive crystals (or grains) of silver halides. When the negative image is projected by the enlarger lens on to the paper, the sensitive silver is affected. On development, those areas which received most light blacken most, those which received least light stay lightest. As the negative was a reversal of the original scene, we now have a negative of a negative, or a positive print. If the negative lacks tonal contrast, it needs a vigorous grade of paper to compensate and give a bright print, full of contrasting tones. Conversely, if the negative has too much contrast, a less vigorous paper will reduce that contrast to normal. Thus, printing papers come in various grades of contrast, usually from 0 to 5. Grade 2 or 3 is considered 'Normal', 0 is softest and 5 is hard and extremely contrasty.

Special paper is available called 'variable contrast'. By using combinations of yellow and magenta filters in the enlarger, the contrast grade of the paper can be adjusted over a wide range.

Economy It is important to read the instructions that come with all chemicals and materials. If the solution is only partly used, and has not been in the dish too long, it can be stored in a full bottle for future use. Stopbath is often supplied with an indicator colour, which changes as the solution becomes exhausted. Fixer, especially, should never be kept beyond the throughput recommended in the instructions, or your prints may fade or discolour.

FILM PROCESSING

Loading the tank Before processing, the film has to be wound into a spiral. This device ensures that no part of the film touches any other part, and the developer, stopbath and fixer have free access to all parts. Most spirals load from the outside towards the centre, though a few load from the core outwards.

(1) In the dark, the shaped leader edge of the film is cut off, and the film gently pushed into the spiral. The instructions with each tank show how this is done.
(2) The spiral is then placed inside the tank and the light-tight lid clipped on.
(3) The light can then be switched on. Loading is greatly simplified if practised

THE DEVELOPING TANK

Film must be loaded in the dark, but you can process in daylight.

first in room lighting with waste film.

Time and temperature To ensure that the negatives will be of the right density and contrast to provide good prints, it is necessary to develop by what is known as time and temperature. Both density and contrast increase as development progresses, and the rate of increase is also affected by (a) the temperature of the developer, and (b) the amount of agitation given to the solution. The warmer the developer, the quicker it acts. Similarly, constant agitation, by inverting the tank, speeds development. Most manufacturers recommend 10 seconds initial agitation when the developer is poured in, followed by 5 seconds every minute. This is equivalent to inverting the tank and righting it once.

Procedure If the instructions recommend, say, 9 minutes development at 20°C (68°F), proceed as follows:

(1) Have developer, stopbath and fixer ready in three beakers.
(2) Check temperatures with the thermometer, rinsing it thoroughly after each check to ensure that no stopbath or fixer comes into contact with the developer.
(3) Pour developer into the loaded tank and start timing the process.
(4) Agitate the tank for 10 seconds initially to release any air bubbles, then for 5 seconds per minute.
(5) 10 seconds or so before development is complete, pour out the developer, and begin to pour in the stopbath just as development time is completed.
(6) Agitate continuously for 1 minute, then pour out the stopbath and replace it with the fixer.
(7) Agitate continuously until fixation is complete; usually 2-3 minutes but it varies according to the make of fixer.
(8) Wash for 10 minutes with the open tank under running water, then hang to dry in a dust-free atmosphere. Film-wiper tongs will remove excess moisture, speed drying, and help ensure a clean film.

PRINTING AND CONTACTING

Printing from a negative Because our camera produced a negative – that is, an image of the original scene with the tones reversed – we now have to produce a reversal of the negative. That is, a print with the tones the right way round, with sky a light tone, shadows dark, and so on. A negative may be pressed into contact with a sheet of printing paper, exposed to light and developed, but the image is too small for general viewing and display. So we enlarge it.

The enlarger The modern enlarger is rather like your camera. The negative is inserted in a carrier beneath an illuminated lamp-house. The enlarger head is then raised to give the desired amount of enlargement, and the lens is focused until the image projected on the baseboard is clear and sharp.

When the negative image is viewed on the enlarger baseboard or the paper-masking frame, the desired grade of paper is selected, and the enlarger lamp is switched off. The paper is then loaded into the masking frame, the enlarger is switched on to project an image of the negative for the required duration of exposure, and then the paper is developed.

Making contact sheets If a 36-exposure 35mm film is cut into six strips of six negatives each, the whole film can be printed on a single sheet of 20×25cm (8×10in) paper. Normally, the negatives are pressed into contact with the sheet of paper and exposed to either room lighting or the light from the enlarger. A soft grade of paper is advisable for black and white contacting, as it copes with negatives of varying density. Such a sheet of contact prints helps you select the best pictures for enlarging. Contact-print sheets can also be made from colour negative films, or even from a selection of colour slides, provided that the appropriate colour paper is used.

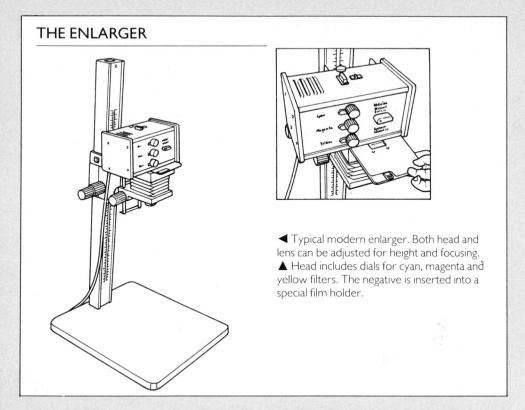

THE ENLARGER

◄ Typical modern enlarger. Both head and lens can be adjusted for height and focusing.
▲ Head includes dials for cyan, magenta and yellow filters. The negative is inserted into a special film holder.

Masking frames Unless the printing paper is held flat on the baseboard of the enlarger, the edges or centre may curve up and the image will be clear and sharp only in parts of the print. To avoid this, a masking frame is used. The masking frame is adjustable to the size of the paper being used, such as 12.5×17.5cm (5×7in), 20×25cm (8×10in), and so on. The arms of the frame hold the paper by the edges only, and after processing the paper will have neat white borders where the edges were masked. Masking frames are available in larger sizes up to 40×50cm (16×20in), but 20×25cm (8×10in) is convenient for most amateur purposes. One type has a magnetic base and movable metal corners, by means of which a borderless print can be made.

Dish development It is essential to have three dishes for black-and-white paper development, one for developer, one

for stopbath and one for fixer. Always work from left to right or from right to left. The paper is slid under the surface of the developer with one smooth motion and the dish is then gently rocked, back and forth and from side to side. The key work here is 'gently'. This ensures that the image develops evenly, without streaking. Just before the end of development the print is lifted by one corner, drained, and transferred to the stopbath for a few seconds, then lifted and drained again, and transferred to the fixer. After fixation the print is transferred to the wash water.

Adding a sky Sometimes a pleasant landscape picture is spoiled by the absence of a good cloud formation or, at worst, there is a blank sky. In such a case, it is possible to 'print in' the sky from another negative. Indeed, some photographers collect negatives of good sky effects just for this purpose. You start by composing the landscape picture the way you want it, using a sheet of plain writing or typing paper in the masking frame. On this you pencil the horizon line. A small strip of printing paper is then exposed and developed, to determine the correct exposure for the foreground. The negative carrier is then removed from the enlarger, and the negative replaced with one containing a suitable sky. Its image is enlarged and adjusted until it looks natural above the horizon line you have drawn. Again, a test exposure is made.

A sheet of printing paper is now inserted in the masking frame, and the red filter swung across the enlarger lens (because the paper is not affected by red light, this enables you to observe the image without an exposure being made). Now hold a sheet of card midway between the lens and masking frame so as to cast a shadow across the bottom half of the paper – that is, the landscape foreground. Use the horizon line on the plain paper to locate the upper limit of the shadow. Then swing the red filter to one side and make the correct exposure for the sky, moving the card gently, just 2.5cm (1in) either way, to prevent the formation of a hard, tell-tale edge to the landscape exposure. Now replace the sky negative with that of the landscape and, using the same technique, expose for the foreground. If the sky on the landscape is blank it will be dark on the negative, so for this part of the operation it will not be necessary to shade the sky area with the card.

High-contrast printing The appearance of a black-and-white print can often be vastly improved by using a high-contrast printing paper – say, grade 5. If, for example, the picture contained a great deal of foliage taken under dull lighting conditions, the many twigs and leaves would merge into a mass of similar shades of grey. By using a high-contrast printing paper, the effect of a line etching is achieved, with all the minute detail standing out in good contrast.

Toning It is quite easy to apply sepia toning to modern black-and-white prints. Simple kits are available complete with instructions. Blue and green toners are also available.

Converging verticals When the camera is tilted upwards, the verticals of buildings tend to converge. This phenomenon is acceptable to many viewers, but is considered unpleasant or unnatural by others. Converging verticals can be corrected as follows: one side of the enlarging paper mask is tilted upwards until the verticals appear parallel again. The image is then re-focused at the centre, and the enlarging lens stopped well down so the whole image is sharp.

Storage of chemicals (1) Developers keep longer in dark-glass bottles. They will, however, deteriorate if the bottles are only partly filled. To get around this problem, buy a number of bottles of different sizes, especially 600ml (1 pint) and 1000ml (2 pints) for storing part-used developers, filling each to the brim. Another way around this problem is to buy aerosols of inert gas. A squirt of this will fill the air space in a part-filled bottle and prevent oxidation.

Choosing fixers Fixers for films are usually more concentrated than those used for papers, so it is false economy to use a film-strength fixer for papers. Moreover, paper fixer is generally used in an open dish, where it can attract dust, hairs and so on. If the same solution is then used for fixing a film, these bodies may adhere to the drying emulsion, resulting in spots and hair-lines on the prints.

Variable-contrast paper The advantage of this type of paper is that different grades of contrast are obtainable simply by using yellow and magenta filters, singly or in combination, on the enlarger, making it unnecessary to buy packets of paper of different grades.

COLOUR TRANSPARENCIES

The tank Almost all tanks used by amateurs today are made of plastic and are impervious to the chemicals used in photography. The same tank will serve for both black and white and colour films, provided scrupulous cleanliness is maintained. Stainless steel tanks are also available, but these are best used for black-and-white processing, as most become badly discoloured when in contact with colour chemicals. The discoloration may contain residues that could cause unwanted colour casts in subsequent colour films. The popular plastic tanks will also fit the auto-rotating processors (see below), which is not possible with stainless steel tanks.

Chemicals Practically all modern slide films can be processed in Kodak's E-6 chemistry. Thus, they are termed 'E-6 compatible'. Basically, the succession of chemical stages are: (1) first developer, (2) reversal bath (to change the image from negative to positive), (3) colour developer, (4) bleach-fix. Other firms produce packs of similar chemicals. Two of these, Photo Technology Chrome Six and Paterson 3E6, incorporate the reversal bath in the colour developer, reducing the process to three chemical stages.

Similarly, packs of chemicals for colour-negative films are available following the basic Kodak C-41 process, which has the following chemical stages: (1) developer, (2) bleach, (3) fixer, (4) stabilizer. Most photo shops also stock a simplified version of C-41 chemistry, in which the bleach and fixer are combined and the stabilizer eliminated, leaving (1) developer, (2) bleach-fix. With an additive, the same chemicals can be used to process printing papers compatible with the Kodak Ektaprint 2 process. Photo Technology Photocolor II includes a bottle of this additive, while in Paterson 2NA (which means two bath no additive) the extra ingredient is incorporated in the two solutions.

For making prints directly from slides you can use Ilford Cibachrome paper and associated chemicals, or Kodak Ektachrome 14 paper processed in Ektaprint R14 chemical. Again most photo shops stock non-proprietary versions of these processes.

Ancillary equipment A really good thermometer will serve for both colour and black-and-white processing. Choose a thermometer specifically marked for colour. Firms such as Jobo and Paterson now supply auto-rotating processors. In these a water jacket and the various chemicals contained in bottles are maintained at a precise temperature. The tank containing the film, or a similar drum containing colour paper, is held in the processor and rotated at a precise speed in the water jacket, ensuring exact temperature control at each chemical stage.

Cleanliness As successful colour processing depends on meticulous adherence to routine coupled to scrupulous cleanliness, follow these rules:

(1) Equip yourself with a reliable timekeeper. A proper darkroom clock has a sweep second hand and is easier to read than a wristwatch. Any large clock is suitable, provided the minutes and seconds can be accurately read.
(2) Have everything to hand and laid out in the right order before you start.
(3) Rely on accuracy, not luck!
(4) If the instructions call for a one-minute wash, a quick dip is not enough. The slightest trace of chemical carried over to the next bath will cause unwanted colour casts – or even total disaster.
(5) The tank, the film spiral, bottle caps, thermometer, and chemical containers must be *thoroughly* washed after use to avoid any trace of contamination.

Following such a routine will pay dividends in trouble-free processing, leading to excellent negatives, prints and slides which can be printed effortlessly.

PROCESSING/ACCESSORIES

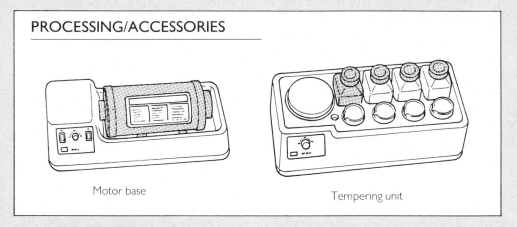

Motor base

Tempering unit

DRUM PROCESSING

Drums and tanks Just as a film is loaded into a tank for processing, so a sheet of colour paper is loaded into a drum. In fact, the paper drum, which is cylindrical and made of plastic, looks just like a tank designed to hold several films. Unlike the film, however, the paper does not have to be fed into a spiral, but presses against the inner wall of the drum. Today colour paper can be processed at room temperature, whereas a few years ago a temperature as high as 38°C (100°F) was required. It is no longer necessary to have thermostatic control of solution temperatures outside and inside the drum. Instead, the drum is rolled back and forth on the bench during the successive stages: (1) water for pre-heating the drum, (2) developer, (3) stopbath, (4) bleach-fix, (5) wash.

With the drum rolled on its side, as little as 50ml (2 fl oz) of each solution is needed for a single sheet of 20×25cm (8×10in) paper.

Preparation of chemicals Until recently as many as six liquids and powders were needed to make up a set of colour-processing solutions. Nowadays the job is simpler and ready-to-dilute liquid concentrates are the order of the day. The following are the chemical stages needed for the various colour processes:

(1) Colour negative: (a) developer, (b) bleach-fix.
(2) Colour print from negative: (a) developer, (b) bleach-fix.
(3) Colour-slide film: (a) first developer, (b) colour developer (containing reversal agent), (c) bleach-fix.
(4) Colour print from colour slide, using Cibachrome process: (a) developer, (b) bleach, (c) fixer.
(5) Colour print from colour slide, using Ektaprint R14 process: (a) first developer, (b) stopbath, (c) colour developer, (d) bleach-fix, (e) stabiliser. Equivalent processes with only three chemical stages are available from independent manufacturers, and are stocked by most photo shops.

TEMPERATURE CONTROL

Accurate temperature This comes first in all processing, especially of colour-slide film. Here are some tips for getting and maintaining the right temperature:
(1) Ask your dealer for a colour thermometer, which is more accurate than ordinary types.
(2) Even with black-and-white film, do *not* pour warm developer into a cold tank. Warm the tank first, by standing it in a bowl of water at the processing temperature.
(3) A tank containing colour film, or a drum containing colour paper, needs to be

pre-warmed. If it is not, the temperature of the solution will drop as it is poured in. To overcome this, the instructions for the process usually include a nomograph. This tells you the required temperature of the pre-heating water that should be poured in for the first minute: it varies according to the ambient temperature of the darkroom.

(4) Some colour processes are now panthermic – that is, they can be carried out at lower temperatures than formerly; in some cases little more than room temperature is required and this is easily maintained. The processing time will be longer at the lower temperature, but this allows a far greater margin for error. For instance, a timing error of half a minute represents 20 per cent of a processing time of 2½ minutes but only 5 per cent of 10 minutes. In the former case it could result in severe under- or over-development, but in the latter its effect would be insignificant.

Thermo-units   Apart from the automatic print processors with thermostatic control already mentioned, there are other ways of maintaining even temperature during processing. A separate thermostat and water heater can be purchased and used in a convenient receptacle: In such a set-up it is necessary to move the water around occasionally so that temperature remains even in all parts of the vessel. Even the heater and thermostat used for fish tanks may be suitable for colour processing at lower temperatures.

Wash water   With most colour processes the temperature of the water used for rinses between the chemical stages should be fairly close to that of the chemical solutions. This may entail having a large bucket of warm water standing in the sink or nearby. The temperature can be maintained with an occasional splash from the hot tap or a kettle. Special 9-litre (2 gal) buckets with extra space for mixing are available.

If you process black-and-white film in cold weather, lower the temperature of the final wash water two or three degrees at a time, for periods of half a minute, until tap temperature is reached. This can be done by pouring from a jug into the tank, then topping up the jug with tap water.

Polaroid   This has already been described in the Film chapter (see page 111). Briefly, there are three types – for ordinary colour slides, for black-and-white slides of normal tone, and for high-contrast black-and-white slides. Processing is carried out in room lighting in a small machine.

COLOUR NEGATIVES

Simple processing   A black-and-white film requires only developer, stopbath and fixer. A colour negative film is just as easy to process, the three stages being developer, stopbath and bleach-fix. Bleach-fix serves a double purpose: fixing the image, and removing the unwanted dye present in the filter layers of the film. Typical chemical stages for colour films and papers are given under Preparation of chemicals, page 117.

Ancillary equipment   Three things are required to ensure perfect film processing. First is a reliable thermometer. Make sure the dealer offers you one suitable for colour processing. Second, you need a pair of film-wiper tongs. This will remove all surplus water from the emulsion after processing, leaving spotless negatives. Third, choose the most dust-free room in the house for drying the film. This is usually the bathroom. If dust or hairs adhere to the emulsion while drying, these will appear as white spots or lines on the finished print.

Home or away   There is no financial advantage to be gained by processing colour-negative films at home. Even without wastage, the price of an amateur chemistry kit is such that each film

developed will cost almost as much, and sometimes more, than is charged by a commercial processing house. Nevertheless, by processing your film at home you get something extra – excitement, a sense of achievement, and the chance to see your negative shortly after the pictures are taken.

Step by step   Having prepared the three solutions (developer, stopbath, and bleach-fix) for processing your colour-negative film, the process is as follows:

(1)   Stand the film tank, with the film inside, in a dish to collect any drops that may be spilled.
(2)   Check the temperature of the developer. When it is correct, pour it into the tank and start the clock. Snap on the tank-port cap and apply the initial agitation given in the instructions.
(3)   As the development time draws to a close, pour out the developer. Pour in the stopbath just as the clock indicates that development is complete. Agitate occasionally for the required period, usually a minute.
(4)   At the end of the period, pour out the stopbath and pour in the bleach-fix; fixation takes about six to eight minutes.
(5)   When the time is up, pour out the bleach-fix, wash the film, and hang it up to dry.

Print washers   You can buy a high-speed print washer which provides a constant flow of water through a tray. Plastic dividing pegs keeps prints of different sizes in place.

Dry and file   A wet film usually has an inward curl but flattens as it dries. Even when it appears fairly hot to the touch, it may still hold a slight amount of moisture and a further half-hour's drying will do no harm. In a proper film dryer, a bone dry film can be obtained after only seven to ten minutes. The film should then be cut into strips and filed.

PRINTING

Contact sheet This consists of six 35mm strips, each of six negatives (i.e. 36 exposures), printed together on a single sheet of 20×25cm (8×10in) paper. This can be filed alongside the negative sheet in an album, either colour contacts, or some photographers are satisfied with contacting on ordinary black and white enlarging paper. At all events, a contact sheet enables you quickly to locate and select your best pictures.

Filtration and analysers Colour negatives have an all-over orange tinge which makes it difficult to observe the colours on the film, which are the reverse of those in the original subject. (A red object, for example, is green on the negative.) The orange tinge is, in fact, a mask. Its job is to correct for the imperfections in the dyes used to form the image. In simple terms, the head of the colour enlarger has dials for yellow, magenta and cyan filters which can be introduced into the light path in controllable amounts. For printing from colour negatives only yellow and magenta are needed (cyan is used only when printing from slides), but the right combination must be chosen if the colours in the finished print are to look natural.

The correct balance of filters is achieved by means of an analyser, though you will find that, with experience, you can make a fairly accurate guess. To use the analyser, a diffuser is put in front of the enlarger lens to 'scramble' the image. The dials of the analyser are then turned until a diode indicates that the depth (value) of each filter is right for that particular negative. A simple analyser may cost about £50; an analyser/meter, which will also indicate the correct exposure for each print, may cost at least four times as much.

Exposure and meters The correct enlarging exposure depends on four things: the sensitivity or 'speed' of the paper; the illumination in the enlarger; the lens

COLOUR METER

A colour and exposure analyser makes printing from colour negatives very much easier, and can virtually eliminate repeated test exposures.

aperture chosen (it is easier to be consistent if the lens is always stopped down the same amount — for instance, two or three values down from maximum aperture); and the total density of the filter pack. 'Filter pack' is a term describing the combined filtration you have dialled in, such as 50Y 20M (50 yellow and 20 magenta values). The term originated in the days when it was common practice to combine small sheets of filters into a pack for insertion in a drawer in the enlarger head, between lamp and negative. Only the cheapest enlargers still work on this system.

Naturally, the denser the filter pack, the less light will reach the paper and the longer will be the exposure required. This can be determined by means of a test strip. A small sheet of paper is uncovered, in sections of an inch at a time, for about five seconds per section; in other words, each section will have been exposed for five seconds longer than the section that follows it. After development, the best exposure can be selected and the final print made.

An exposure meter does the job automatically. Placed on the masking frame, it measures the total light coming through the lens, and indicates the right exposure. A simpler type tries to maintain the same exposure from print to print. The lens is

opened and closed until the standard exposure is achieved. Lenses perform least well at wide apertures, so the former type of meter is often preferable.

A ring-around This is a printed sheet of pictures designed to help you decide whether your colour prints have a natural colour or contain what is known as a cast. When a colour print is made, it should ideally have a pleasing similarity to the colours of the original subject. In many cases, though, there will be a cast towards yellow, magenta, cyan, red, blue or green which needs to be corrected in the next print from the same negative.

At the centre of the ring-around is a small picture of good colour. This is called neutral. There will then be series of pictures radiating from the centre, like a six-pointed star. Each 'ray' will have perhaps four pictures with a particular colour cast, progressively more pronounced the farther they are from the centre. The yellow pictures, for example, will be marked with values such as 05Y, 10Y, 20Y, 40Y. Other casts will be similarly marked. When you have decided on the cast value of your print, you can read off the amount of corrective filtration required, and this is dialled into the enlarger's filtration controls. These are continuous, usually covering about 0-130 values of yellow, magenta and cyan.

SPECIAL TECHNIQUES

Shading and burning-in Part of a print can be darkened or lightened by giving more or less exposure to a given area. For example, a sky can be darkened by giving it extra exposure while shading the foreground with a card. An area that appears too dark can be shaded during part of the exposure by means of a dodger, which is a small piece of card fixed to a thin wire handle.

Colour control We have already seen how a ring-around, used in conjunction with the filters in the enlarger head, helps to correct colour casts and produce a print of pleasing colour. There is, in fact, no need to aim always for a true colour rendering. If, for example, the original scene looks rather cold and sunless, extra yellow can be added. This is done by *reducing* the yellow value in the filter pack when negative materials are used, or by *adding* yellow in the case of reversal papers. Similarly, extra blue may be added to produce a moody effect.

Using effect filters on the enlarger There are now many effect-filter systems available for cameras, producing graduated colour effects, star-bursts, multiple images, and many others. Few photographers think of using the same filters on the enlarger lens, and yet this can produce highly creative, weird and sometimes humorous effects. Because of the smaller size of most enlarger lenses, some effect accessories have minimal effect, and you would need to experiment with these. With graduated and centre-spot filters, for example, the best effects will be obtained with the lens at full aperture, and this may lead to very short exposures. For the keen darkroom worker, the variety of results that you can obtain is well worth the effort.

Multi-mask Makers such as Paterson and Jobo provide a multi-mask which acts

MULTI-MASKS

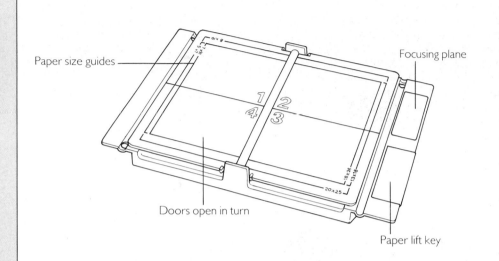

Paper size guides

Focusing plane

Doors open in turn

Paper lift key

▲ This multi-mask is designed to hold several different sizes of paper, and the paper size guides on the white upper surface aid framing. The focusing plane at the right of the mask is a white panel positioned in the same plane as the paper surface (focusing on the raised light-tight cover would produce a blurred image on the print). The paper-lift key makes it easier to remove the exposed paper without marking.

◄ The four doors of the mask can be opened in turn to make the exposure. Closed doors are light-tight, so you can make four completely separate prints on a single sheet of paper.

as a normal masking frame, giving a white 20×25cm (8×10in) border to paper, but also serving an equally important purpose. Various sections of the mask can be uncovered independently, so that four 10×15cm (4×5in) test or finished prints may be made on a single sheet of 20×25cm (8×10in) paper. This is also useful for making a series of test exposures in steps from the same image – when printing in colour, you can use a different filter pack for each picture and see which works best. One type has five separate 'fingers' which can be lifted one at a time to give successively increasing exposures.

PRINTS FROM SLIDES

Internegs and reversal prints There are two ways to obtain a colour print from a colour slide. The one most often used is to photograph the slide on colour negative film, and from this negative to print on colour paper in the normal way. Because such a negative represents an intermediate stage between slide and print, it is called an interneg. The second way is to put the colour slide in the enlarger and make a print directly. This calls for the use of reversal-type colour paper such as Ilford's Cibachrome range.

Internegs Commercial or by copier? An interneg can be made by a commercial house so cheaply that is is hardly worth the amateur's while to produce one. The enthusiast, however, will want to have a go, using his or her normal colour-negative film. The easiest method is to use a slide-copying device containing its own lens, the body of an automatic single-lens reflex camera being fitted at one end and the slide to be copied at the other. Some of these copiers, such as the Panagor and the Ohnar, have an adjustment permitting just a part of the slide to be enlarged to the full 35mm frame. With daylight-type film, the copier is simply held up to the sky, preferably when some sunshine and clouds are present, judgement of the exposure being left to the automatic metering of the camera.

Reversal papers Ektachrome paper will give a print directly from a slide, and has the advantage of not increasing the contrast of the original. In recent years Cibachrome paper has become popular, owing to its clean whites and to the fact that the colours fade far less than on most other papers. With Cibachrome, though, there is a slight tendency towards an increase in contrast, so that best results are obtained with slides of modest contrast.

Lighting and colour balance A colour film is balanced to give good results with *either* daylight *or* tungsten light, and this is marked on the carton. If daylight film is exposed in tungsten light without a compensating filter, the result will be reddish; if an artificial-light film is exposed to daylight without a compensating filter, the result will be very blue. With the recent introduction of ultra-fast films, the situation has changed slightly. Pictures taken with these fast films in mixed lighting, as in a room artificially lit but with daylight coming through a window at the side, give more pleasing results than are obtainable with slower films.

FINISHING

Drying the film The sensitive emulsion of the film is protected by a layer of super-coating, which helps prevent damage caused by accidental touching of the film, particularly in its wet stages. Even so, touching with the fingers, especially fingernails, or against the workbench, may still cause scratching unless great care is taken. The rule is to handle the film only by its edges, never gripped between the fingers. The film will also pick up hairs and dust if left to dry for too long in a damp atmosphere, or if people are constantly moving to and fro.

Drying prints Most amateurs nowadays use RC (resin-coated) papers. In these, the very thin sensitive sheet is protected on both sides by a thin plastic coating. This allows quicker access by the chemicals and much faster washing times than when fibre-based papers are used. Washing time may be only 4 minutes for RC papers but 30 minutes for fibre-based ones, in running water. If wiped free from surface moisture and stood in a record rack, RC prints will dry flat. Double-weight fibre-based papers may be wiped and laid face-up on absorbent paper or other material, but single-weight glossy fibre-based papers are glazed in contact with a chromium sheet in a drying press.

Borders and blades Most paper masks used to hold the printing paper while enlarging cover the edges of the paper, leaving a white border. Such borders are acceptable if the print is to be hand-held and unmounted, but needs to be trimmed away if the print is to be mounted. The cleanest way to do this without special equipment is to put the print face-up on a piece of stout cardboard, such as artboard, and trim the edges off using a steel ruler and a craft knife. Chemists as well as hobby shops sell scalpels with detachable blades in packets of six. Buy the blades with a long point.

Trimmers Quicker than a ruler and scalpel is a trimmer specially made for the job. These come in two types. In the desk type, the edge of the print is pushed under a clear acetate guard and the sloping top board is gently pressed down against a spring to lower the blade. More popular are wheel trimmers. In these the print is held square to the trimming edge, a circular steel blade attached to a hand grip. This is simply slid along to trim off the white border.

MOUNTS AND MOUNTING

The modern mount The very ornate mounts of yesteryear are still made, but are seldom purchased these days. Print presentation in most camera clubs and exhibitions is now almost entirely limited to plain white or cream mounts. The print itself is mounted flush with the edge of the mount, or with several inches of mount forming a border, wider at the bottom than at the sides and top. If the edges of the print happen to be rather light, it is common practice to 'separate' the print from the mount by drawing a black line round it with a felt-tip pen.

Stick it flat! Most pastes and mountants used in offices are water-based and, if applied to the back of a photographic print, tend to make it swell so that it will not lie quite flat on the mount. Special photographic mountants are available, including one which is simply sprayed on to the back of the print and the mount. Properly applied, with the print then rolled down on to the mount with the aid of a ruler, these work very well. Even better, but more expensive, is a dry-mounting press. A sheet of dry-mounting tissue is tacked with a small iron to the back of the print, which is then positioned on the mount and placed in the press for a few seconds. Secondhand mounting presses are sometimes advertised by professional photography dealers.

STORAGE AND DISPLAY

STORING YOUR PICTURES

Albums with sleeves If you send your films away for processing, they will come back in some kind of envelope or sleeve; provided you mark these and file them consecutively in a drawer, it will never take very long to find the ones you want. There is no doubt, though, that the filing albums you can buy in photo shops afford better protection and give readier access to the negatives you want. The negatives are held in strips in transparent sheets. If each of these has its own sheet of contact prints, choosing negatives and marking off the areas to be printed is easily carried out without handling the negatives themselves.

Contact sheets A single sheet of 20×25cm (8×10in) printing paper will hold 36 35mm negatives, cut into six strips of six, or a 120-size film cut into three or four strips. Contact sheets are equally useful in black-and-white or colour and stored next to their related sheet of negatives in the album, make selection of a particular negative easier and safer. Contacting can be done on the baseboard of the enlarger. If its head is always at the same height with the lens stopped down the same amount every time, the required exposure will seldom vary.

Magazine storage As most amateur slides end up in magazines ready for projection, it seems logical to store them the same way. This is certainly the case if you are in the habit of going through your slides carefully and presenting them, perhaps 36 or 50 at a time, as part of a properly programmed show. Apart from those selected for regular viewing there will always be a greater number of 'overs' which need to be stored for later selection. See next section which gives advice on how to store slides.

Slide boxes Every dealer who sells slide projectors also sells special boxes in which 100, 200 or more slides can be filed close together in numbered slots. These are not only economical of space, but are probably the best way of storing slides which are not wanted for immediate projection. These boxes become a self-contained filing system if used in relation to a card file, in which different subject headings are used, such as landscapes, cloudscapes, children at play, and so on. Reference can then be given to the box and slot number of relevant slides.

Albums Twenty transparencies in thin card or plastic mounts are not very heavy, and can be easily filed in albums consisting of special leaves in heavy-quality clear acetate with twenty pockets, one for each mounted slide. Ring-binding at the side is adequate for this type of slide, but if the more sophisticated type of glazed mount is used, it is best to choose a special colour album in which the ring fitting is at the top. Because the leaves are clear, the complete sheet can be taken from the album and laid on a viewing box or held to the light.

Your enprints Replacing the old family albums in which prints are laboriously stuck with photo-corners, are new albums with self-stick pages. These are now offered for sale in High Street stores. Each album page is faced with a dry stick-down sheet. This is simply peeled back, the enprints arranged on the page, and the cover sheet pressed down over them. It is quick and easy, and if you don't like the arrangement, or want to change it at a later date, all you have to do is peel back the sheet, change the page layout, and press down the sheet again.

Filing and finding If you are going to be a really productive photographer, it will be best to start a filing system at the beginning of your career rather than a year or two later, when the task can be quite daunting. A simple but very highly effective system is to keep a job book in which each film is entered under brief descriptive headings with a consecutive number and in chronological order. This is used in association with an index file.

Writing on prints Any type of ink or pencil can be used on fibre-based black-and-white papers, but RC (resin-coated) prints will neither absorb free-flowing or ball-point inks, nor accept pencil. If a ballpoint pen is used, the ink will smudge, even days later. Fine-writing, fibre-tipped pens are available, containing a spirit ink which will adhere and dry almost instantly on resin-coated surfaces, as well as glass and most plastics. These look like ordinary small ballpoints, so do not confuse them with the broader felt-tipped pens used for parcel writing. If there is a print of which you are particularly proud, leave a wide white border at the bottom where you can put your signature with one of these special pens.

Image permanence Black-and-white negatives and prints will last indefinitely if properly processed, but all dyes fade eventually, and those used in colour photographs are no exception. Colour slides should last for a century or so if stored in a cool, dark, dry place, but even in these ideal conditions colour negatives may begin to fade within twenty years. Colour prints will last longer if you display them away from direct sunlight, and in a dry room – don't hang prints over a radiator, as high temperatures accelerate the fading process. If you have to hang prints in adverse conditions, have them framed under glass, and treat the surface of the print with special lacquer to absorb the damaging ultraviolet light.

DISPLAY

Framing it   Taking good pictures is one thing, presenting them is another, and pride of place these days is split between the album and the conventional frame. Frames are available in great variety in most chain stores; the prices vary enormously, so shop around. If you wish to frame a favourite print, take it with you while shopping to ensure that the sizes match and the colour is suitable.

From key-rings to murals   In all hobby magazines you will see advertisements for the incorporation of your own photographs in items ranging from key-rings to giant murals. A well-defined subject, such as a pet or a car, will look fine on a key-ring and could make a useful present, but beware of those murals. Some of them have an attractively bargain price, but are printed on cheap-looking paper.

Laminates and canvas bonding   The British firm Ademco has recently introduced a series of laminate tissues. When one of these is pressed down on to a photograph with a smooth surface, it is given a textured surface. Initially supplied for professional use, packs of these Ademco laminates should soon be available through amateur photographic shops.

Table viewers   Having produced a set of 24 or 36 exciting slides, you will want to view them without delay, and it is not always convenient to set up a slide projector on its stand and black out a room. Even for the keen-eyed, a 35mm slide is too small for direct viewing and a table viewer is the handiest and best means of examining the slides or showing them to friends. The very simplest type of viewer depends on daylight or room lighting, which is often adequate but on occasions can be irritatingly dim. For a few pounds more you can obtain one of the battery-operated viewers, which have a magnifying lens at the front.

Projectors   According to cost, a modern slide projector for amateur use will have some or all of the following facilities. A remote control handset by means of which slides can be changed forward and backwards, plus remote focusing. Re-focusing is necessary with unglazed mounts, as the film buckles out of the plane of focus as it warms up. More sophisticated units have an autofocus mechanism which, by means of a servo-motor, re-focuses each time a slide pops out of register. The projector will take either straight magazines holding 36 to 50 slides each, or rotary magazines which hold about 80 slides. Among makers of amateur equipment, straight magazine types seem to be preferred. An 85mm lens is considered standard.

Daylight-viewing attachment   This is a device used in conjunction with a slide projector, but not requiring the room to be darkened. Its big advantage is that the image, usually about 20×25cm (8×10in), is easier to view by the whole family at one time. There are two types. One is a bookform stand which incorporates a mirror held at 45° to the projector lens, and a ground-glass back-projection screen; it is set up at right-angles to the projector lens and about 30cm (1ft) away from it. The other device attaches to the front of the projector but requires the lens to be exchanged for a shorter focal length.

Light box and sorting desk   This is a useful device, and some would insist that it is indispensable, especially to the photographer who takes his slide projection seriously. Basically it is an opal translucent surface lit from behind, on which a number of slides can be examined and sorted, ready for correct placing in a magazine. Warning: there is one cheap type whose small tungsten lamps inside create a great deal of heat, which will buckle slides if they remain in position for more than a few minutes. The best kinds have fluorescent tubes which remain cool.

A word for beginners   A good slide show is characterized by three things. First, it holds the audience's interest right to the end. Second, it entertains or informs the audience. Third, it should be seen under comfortable conditions.

One projector   Because of the vast amount of audio-visual equipment on the market, many novices are led to believe that a good slide show can only be presented with a thousand pounds' worth of equipment. This is not the case. With careful selection and preparation, a brilliant slide show can be given with just one projector. The modern projector blacks out momentarily between slides and continuity is maintained with a careful combination of commentary and music.

Commentary   Keep a brief note on your travels of names and places, as well as interesting information about the subjects you take. Later, when arranging your slides for a programme, rehearse what you are going to say with your notes, so that on the night you will be word perfect.

Music by hand   The addition of suitable music will greatly enhance your slide programme, but does not call for expensive equipment. You can have a tape recorder with a suitable piece of music of the right length standing beside the projector position. You can 'play in' with the music, then turn down the volume when you start to speak. If there is a short sequence of particularly beautiful slides which call for no spoken commentary, you can turn up the volume again as you stop speaking.

Silence is golden   Even a trained voice of flawless accent will become boring if it continues too long. It is an old saying among experienced projectionists, that the best parts of the commentary are the pauses between speech. Pauses also enable the audience to take in a particularly impressive sequence without distraction.

AUDIO-VISUAL AIDS

Using two projectors This is the simplest form of audio-visual, or A/V as it is known. By means of a dissolve mechanism the picture from one projector fades down on the screen while the image from the other projector is fading up to full power. Audio-visual is not merely a pleasant means of changing slides without a blackout between images, but it can be an exciting and creative medium. The projectors have to be placed side by side or one above the other so that the two lenses are close. This facilitates accurate matching of the margins of the two images on the screen. This is known as obtaining register.

A manual-dissolve unit In its simplest form a dissolve unit consists of two shutters, one being placed in front of each of the two projector lenses. By moving a control lever, the projectionist can close one shutter while the other is opening, and vice versa. In this way one image fades down while the other fades up. At the end of each lever movement a button works the slide-change mechanism of one projector. Other dissolve units work on a rheostat principle, dimming one projector while bringing the other to full power.

A programmer A programmer is connected to both projectors and to a tape or cassette recorder; there are several models by major equipment companies. The programmer receives inaudible signals from the tape as it is running and transmits these alternately to each projector. Each lamp is dimmed and brightened at a variable rate determined by the projectionist, and slide changing is automatic. Most dissolve units have a handset with which the programme is laid down on the tape and the same programmer can be used to dissolve manually.

Pulsing a tape Although there are variations, it is common for programming to be done on a 4-track tape. The first and second tracks are used for left and right stereo sound, voice and music, the fourth track receives the pulses which are signals conveyed to the two projectors by the programmer, while the third track separates the stereo tracks from the signal track and prevents feedback, or sound interference.

Projection accessories Don't buy a good projector and use the dining room table as a stand. It will be too low, making it necessary to point the projector upwards, which gives an elongated 'keystoning' effect on the screen. Do the job properly. As a once-and-for-all outlay, buy a good quality pack-away projection stand, which will also hold the magazines of slides to be projected. A pressurised air bottle can be used to 'sweep' the slides in the magazine just before projection, ensuring a clean presentation. If you are going into full audio-visual, you will also need a programmer, cassette recorder, pre-amplifier and speakers with extension leads. Have as many electronic items as possible from the same maker, thus ensuring compatibility.

Harmony Except when your programme includes an intentionally startling sequence, the combination of slides and music and the way slides dissolve into each other on the screen should follow a few rules of harmony. Greens dissolve beautifully into other quiet colours, such as greens, blues and greys; reds dissolve nicely into pinks, oranges and browns. Dissolve slowly from one calm, pastoral scene to another, but where traffic and busy movement is involved, a faster slide-change and dissolve time are suitable.

How many slides? Just because every slide taken on a trip is correctly exposed doesn't mean that it should find a place in your slide show. Be quite ruthless in your editing. Assuming an average screen time per slide of 6 seconds, which is quite a long time on the screen, plus an average of 3 seconds dissolve time, you have a showing time of 7½ minutes per 50-slot magazine. Two or three magazines, together with short breaks, are adequate for a half-hour show, which is quite long enough for most audiences.

How many minutes? When arranging your slides and deciding on commentary and music, there is no need to start with an estimated programme length to which you must adhere at all costs. Start the work visually, sorting the slides into a harmonious arrangement. This is best done on a light box or by clipping series of 20 slides in transparent filing sheets against a window. While doing this, your mind should be busy with suitable commentary and music which will fit well at different parts of the programme. The harmony of the finished programme, after cutting and rearranging, will decide the number of minutes the programme should run.

Title sequences Neat title slides are not difficult to make using instant rub-down lettering; for a really professional effect, take special care with alignment and spacing before photographing the title onto slow film. However, with a little foresight, you can effortlessly create much more atmospheric titles while you are still on location. Keep your eyes open for subjects that tell a story in words. Road signs are a classic example; if you photograph the sign welcoming visitors to the holiday resort, your audience will be left in no doubt about where you stayed. Place names aren't the only example, though. A picture of a sign saying 'to the airport' is a good way to introduce the concluding sequence of your show. If no ready-made lettering exists, you can always create your own. On a beach, for example, you might choose to scratch titles in the wet sand – take several photographs of the words being washed away by successive waves, and you'll have an instant sequence.

INDEX

Numbers in italic refer to illustrations

ACKNOWLEDGEMENTS

The publishers would like to thank the following for their kind permission to reproduce the photographs in this book.

Action Plus 24-5, 36; Allsport 13; Biofotos/ Heather Angel 68-74; Camerapress 7; Patrick Lichfield 44 left, 44-5; Ken Griffiths 4, 10-11; Susan Griggs Agency/Adam Woolfitt 76-83; Robert Harding/Tony Jones 34 above; Patrick Lichfield 17, 32 left, 41-3, 46-8; Nadia Mackenzie 37; Eamonn McCabe 2-3, 58-67; Alex McNeill 18, 34-5; Jenny Moulton 30; NHPA/ Stephen Dalton 15, 84-93; Gerard Lacz 38-9; Adrian Neville 21; Octopus Publishing Group Picture Library/John Sims 9; Parr-Joyce Partnership/Will Curwen 29; Nikon UK Ltd 93; Colin Walton 8, 10 above, 26, 28, 31; Tim Woodcock 1, 12, 32-3; George Wright 23, 50-7; Zefa Picture Library 14, 16, 19, 20, 22, 27, 38 above.